# Navigating the Maze

## of Energy Efficiency Projects

Jeff Julia

Published by Energy Project Advisors, Austin, TX
www.energyprojectadvisors.com
Ordering Information:
ATTENTION CORPORATIONS, UNIVERSITIES, COLLEGES AND PROFESSIONAL ORGANIZATIONS: Quantity discounts are available on bulk purchases of this book for educational, gift purposes, or as premiums for increasing magazine subscriptions or renewals. For information, please contact Jeff Julia at info@energyprojectadvisors.com
Navigating the Maze/ Jeff Julia. —1st ed.
ISBN 978-0-9984976-1-7
Library of Congress Cataloging-in-Publication Data
Library of Congress Control Number: 2017931462

# DEDICATION

This book is dedicated to all the small business owners who navigate the maze on their own.

# ACKNOWLEDGMENTS

A special, heartfelt thanks to my mother, Linda Julia, who ingrained in me the belief that, "nobody can take your education away from you," and inspired me to carry that message forward through this book. Thank you to Sara Hoagland Hunter, my copy editor, proofreader and mother in-law who inspires me through her writing.

Also, a big thanks to Leslie Watts, my developmental editor, Jim Wilson, my mentor and coach, Kailash Viswanathan for "throwing me into the fire" very early in my career, Mike Doucette for everything you've taught me over the years along with Bob Mirza and Matt Worth for pushing me to be my best.

Finally, I would like to thank my wife Abby for without her patience and support this book would not have been possible.

# PREFACE

Performing energy efficiency upgrades has increasingly become an attractive way to enhance the overall health and operation of businesses and buildings alike. With a variety of providers focusing on every energy consuming system, as well as manufacturers developing cutting edge technologies, the options are seemingly endless. The government, both local and federal, in combination with utility companies, has continued to incentivize energy efficiency upgrades with tax credits, unique financing vehicles and rebates making the financial attractiveness hard to ignore. To learn more about this attractive industry, visit the Department of Energy's website at www.energy.gov/eere.

In a business atmosphere increasingly saturated with "energy saving" products and proposals, even the simplest of energy efficiency projects can contain disastrous oversights. Before you buy, there are six major aspects of energy efficiency projects which require careful scrutiny. If overlooked or not identified at all, oversights on one aspect alone can drain free cash, seize business operations, cause schedule overruns and infuriate tenants, employees and owners alike. After overcoming the high hurdles to approve these projects in the first place, being blindsided after the fact is the last thing you and your team want to experience.

As business professionals and building specialists, your

expertise in and priorities of maintaining both business and building, increasing efficiencies, planning for the future and mitigating risk are always top-of-mind when you reach your desk in the morning.

Throughout this book, we'll follow Joe Stevenson on his journey trying to do just that by using energy efficiency as a strategy in his business. As the story unfolds, a strategy that at first sounded easy enough to deploy successfully, very quickly unravels into something more complicated than he had imagined. With his limited industry knowledge and resources, can he accomplish his goals or will his business collapse as he tries?

## WHY CONSIDER ENERGY EFFICIENCY?

Although your responsibilities may not be to reduce utility expenses, when approached and implemented properly, the pay-offs of performing energy efficiency upgrades are often tremendous. Pay - offs go well beyond the simple benefit of reduced expenses. All components of a business are positively impacted. Increased employee productivity and engagement, lower turnover and absenteeism, increased rental rates, higher occupancy rates, lower service and repair expenses, improved public relations and brand image, increased sales, lower insurance premiums, safer properties, lower operating expenses, higher valuation and increased profitability are just a snapshot of the benefits from performing energy efficiency improvements. Most of these benefits are rarely quantified or communicated up front but they inevitably come to fruition if the projects are approached and implemented properly. They are like finding money under the mattress.

## WHO SHOULD READ THIS BOOK?

If you are responsible for managing a business or a building, then this book is intended for you. If your responsibilities include generating any of the pay-offs listed above, then this book will be a valuable resource for you as well.

If you are simply interested in learning about the wide range of benefits and faults common on energy efficiency projects, this book will provide you with that education.

Throughout this book, you'll learn about the six aspects of energy efficiency projects. These six aspects are not always clearly listed on the project proposal or discussed in the sales presentation, but should always undergo careful inspection. You'll learn to identify the most common oversights and pitfalls of each aspect and emerge well-equipped with the tools and resources you need to successfully navigate the waters of energy efficiency.

## WHAT DOES THIS BOOK NOT COVER?

This book does not recommend any service providers, equipment vendors or technology types nor does it provide specific legal or financial advice. It does not present all of the types of service providers, technology, equipment, energy savings models, tax incentives, utility rebates, industry organizations or certifications or explain power generation.

## WHAT IS THE SCOPE OF THIS BOOK?

This book strictly focuses on the development and decision making phases of energy efficiency projects with particular emphasis placed on the due diligence required to benefit from the six critical aspects every project shares. It establishes a framework for evaluating proposals enabling you to make wise investment decisions, told through the practical story of Joe Stevenson, a restaurant owner experiencing several HVAC related issues. As he begins the process to resolve his issues, he learns that energy efficiency improvements can not only solve his HVAC problems but deliver much more. The events that transpire will guide you through the framework of evaluating all six aspects successfully, pointing out along the way common oversights and costly shortcuts that are often made.

If you find yourself identifying more and more with Joe while reading this book, it is achieving its intent. My aptitude is to help you navigate the development and decision making phases of energy efficiency projects successfully so you can make wise investment decisions. That is our business model. I encourage you to visit our website (www.energyprojectadvisors.com) or give us a call at 512-765-5328 if you would like to learn more.

Full disclosure, at the end of this book, I will tell you how you can hire us to help you with your energy efficiency needs. We do not sell energy efficiency projects or perform energy audits, nor do we represent any providers. Rather, we are committed to empowering you with the tools and resources we've developed from our years working in the energy efficiency industry, allowing you to screen providers, review audits and grade proposals for your business or building.

Please consider this book a gift from Energy Project Advisors and its founder. I have committed my career to helping companies and individuals make informed energy decisions based on their needs and dollars.

If you would like further help on a specific project, then know you have an independent resource you can trust to support you.

## *WHY WAS THIS BOOK WRITTEN?*

I've worked with hundreds of clients over the years who resemble Joe Stevenson and although each has his or her own unique situation, client frustrations are all too similar.

One client in particular has greatly inspired the writing of this book. I offer a bit of background here.

Adam was an owner of a neighborhood full service restaurant and bar in the Boston metro area. When he responded to a mailer from the utility company for a free energy efficiency audit, it was I who responded to his request.

From my initial visit on a cold Monday morning in November, I could tell his business was in a tough spot financially and that Adam was not the type of guy who trusted people at face value. He was very blunt, skeptical, busy and obviously stressed out. I quickly learned he had a wife, newborn, and restaurant that was chronically empty.

After completing my audit, it was clear to me that his restaurant was an ideal candidate for energy efficiency improvements. It seemed like every low cost, high return opportunity existed. I knew the project I developed was going to be a home run, a slam dunk, a "no brainer".

The next week, I returned to present my findings to Adam with proposal in hand. Fortuitously, I was able to present an offer impossible to refuse.

It just so happened the utility company was way behind on their energy saving target for the year. At the last minute, the managers had decided to pay for the full cost of outstanding energy efficiency projects in their small business program with no strings attached. Only a select handful of projects qualified for this deal. These were projects that would save the most energy at the lowest installation cost, earning a 100% utility rebate. The project I had developed for Adam obviously qualified.

The minute Adam and I sat down, I began to understand why his business was in such jeopardy and why there were no customers, and why he suffered from such stress. He put the weight of the world on his back and *refused* to accept help, in all aspects of his operation.

I tried every sales tactic I could to get him to see the light. I walked him through each section of the one page agreement. I explained each improvement and offered to walk him into six other businesses on his street I was working with. I addressed the why, the what, the how, the when, the who.

Every attempt failed, every offer was shot down.

When I drove by his restaurant six months later and saw the "closed" sign I couldn't help but wonder if the momentum and benefits from $30,000 worth of attractive energy efficiency improvements could have saved his business.

His words, "This is too good to be true; what's the catch?" rang in my ears and incentivized me to find a way to build trust with business owners by proving the benefits of honest, well thought out energy efficiency methods.

I knew there were other Adams out there who did not understand or trust the energy efficiency audits and proposals they were shown. This book based on my company's philosophy is my offering to all in search of a trustworthy, objective energy evaluation resource. It is the result of countless hours of learning, strategizing, writing, revising, proofreading, designing and publishing. Just like authoring a book was outside of my expertise, I understand that energy efficiency is outside of most business professionals' expertise. Some folks in the energy efficiency field have been taking advantage of that fact. I, however, have chosen to bridge the gap with this book and my company, Energy Project Advisors.

Why go through all the work to write a book about energy efficiency projects and start a business providing independent review services? Because I empathize with you. Business professionals are time and resource constrained. The marketplace is glutted with energy saving products and proposals resulting in confusion and skepticism across the board.

I am passionate about energy efficiency and understand how painful and counterproductive it can be to have a problem with no resources to solve it. I know how time consuming it is to learn a new skill or area of expertise and how disheartening it is to take a leap of faith, taking a proposal at face value, just to realize in hindsight there were warning signs you failed to heed had you been better informed by a trustworthy resource.

I do not want you to make the same mistakes Joe Stevenson and others like him have made, especially if I can do something to prevent it. I have written this book because I do not want you to endure the headaches and sleepless nights of making a catastrophic decision, wondering what happened, and pondering how you are going to salvage the remnants. I do not want you to lose your job, your livelihood, or your business because the cash flows were unsustainable.

The example of Joe Stevenson, a composite of many former clients and friends, provides you with the tools and resources to avoid the consequences above. In addition, I'd like to answer the most important questions that are not so easily answered by a salesperson positioned to sell you an energy efficiency project. These questions require both industry expertise and an objective perspective:

1. Am I approaching energy efficiency the right way?
2. Does this proposal align with my needs and goals?
3. What metrics should I use to determine if this is a good project?
4. The proposal is too technical; how do I translate the jargon to make sense of it?
5. Is there a resource available to provide me with an honest appraisal of this proposal?
6. How do I know the provider is reputable?
7. How do I verify that I will get what I pay for?
8. Will the equipment require ongoing maintenance to perform efficiently?
9. How were the savings developed? Can I trust them?
10. What are utility rebates? Why does the utility company offer these?
11. What are tax incentives? Does the project qualify for them?
12. This sounds too good to be true; is it?
13. I don't want to use my own cash for this project, what other options are available?
14. How can I increase the probability this investment will perform as predicted? Or better yet, outperform the predictions?
15. What other benefits will this project provide that we'd like to achieve?

By providing you with the answers to these questions, the intent of this book is to prepare you to evaluate with confidence the claims of any energy efficiency provider offering you products and services. My goal is for you to be able to speak intelligently and to maximize the chance that the proposal will meet your needs and exceed projections. The six aspects outlined should significantly reduce your risks and empower you to make wise investment decisions.

## *WHAT QUALIFIES ME?*

After working on roughly $500M in energy efficiency projects, I believe there is a big difference between certifications and qualifications. I've spent my career pursuing qualifications that allow me to be of maximum value in the energy efficiency industry.

While earning my mechanical engineering degree at Northeastern University in Boston, MA, I developed a passion for energy efficiency. After graduating, I started developing my qualifications on the campuses of colleges and universities around New England.

Most of my time was invested in construction management activities, developing an understanding of what exactly happens once an energy efficiency project is underway. I learned about the energy consuming systems (heating, ventilation, cooling, water, lighting, building envelope, controls, etc.) in all kinds of campus buildings, interacted daily with the contractors installing the projects and provided project updates at weekly client meetings.

I spent a lot of time in mechanical rooms, where most HVAC equipment is housed, and asked a lot of questions of both the contractors and my superiors – industry veterans. Soon I could determine exactly what systems existed, how they were functioning and what improvements could be made among the vast range of options.

As I spent more and more time in campus buildings like ice skating rinks, gymnasiums, dormitories, administration offices, academic classrooms, dining halls and research laboratories, my understanding of the unique energy efficiency opportunities in each grew so I began developing projects myself. I then joined an energy efficiency start-up as its ninth employee, giving me the opportunity to wear many hats. I became responsible for performing building audits and identifying the energy saving opportunities, creating the energy savings models and crunching the numbers, developing the scopes of the projects and sourcing pricing from equipment vendors and contractors, quantifying the utility rebates and filing the applications, managing installations and performing functional tests after the installations were complete.

To provide some context, allow me summarize a few of the projects I was involved with. If this is too technical, I apologize in advance.

On the campus of Clark University in Worcester, MA, a LEED certified life sciences building was operating well above its energy use requirements. After auditing the building and reviewing the construction documents, it turned out the energy management systems (EMS) were not tested after being installed. There were two, and neither was working correctly.

An energy management system is like the brain of a building. It is a computer based system that automatically controls the HVAC systems, performing operations like turning equipment on and off, deciding whether to cool or heat the building, adjusting room temperatures based on the time of day and day of the week, etc. The EMS for the laboratories was not communicating with the EMS for the lobbies, hallways, offices and classrooms. The daylighting controls (sensors that dim the lights per amount of sunlight) were not even connected. They were installed but never connected or tested. To resolve these issues, we brought the controls technicians back in to correct the oversights, then monitored the building's energy usage over the next several months.

On a different campus in Massachusetts, Babson College, one of the highest energy consuming buildings was an ice skating rink. Upon investigating, the rink's HVAC system was found to have multiple problems with a heating system that was trying to warm the building at the same time the cooling system was trying to cool it down. Additionally, the building was not zoned properly, meaning, there were no air-proof walls and doors separating the cold spaces (the ice skating rink itself) from the heated spaces (the locker rooms and press boxes). And finally, the largest exterior wall, running the entire length of the ice skating rink, contained absolutely zero insulation. So, on a hot summer day, a single piece of sheet metal separated the outdoors from the twenty-degree ice skating rink. I successfully worked to attain solutions to these problems.

For Brandeis University, while I was completing a lighting audit in another LEED certified life sciences building, I noticed the fume hood fans, where the students would perform their experiments, were running at full speed despite the building being vacant.

Fume hoods are like big vacuum cleaners that consume a lot of energy. Conventional energy saving systems for fume hoods are very expensive. With a little creativity and energy efficiency prowess, I was able to have a contractor install occupancy sensors, that are typically used to turn off lights, to reduce the fans' speed when the laboratories were unoccupied. This unique project required a small amount of custom coding in the EMS to function as intended but was so financially advantageous, the client happily agreed to the improvement.

In total, I was involved with over $3.5M worth of projects on a dozen campuses around New England including Brown University, Phillips Andover Academy and

Worcester Polytechnic Institute (WPI).

With a strong foundation built upon a wide variety of building types, energy consuming systems, and energy efficiency improvements, I then joined a company that developed energy efficiency projects for utility companies in New England. In some parts of the country these companies are known as third party implementers. In others, they are known as ESCO's (energy service companies). With this company, I was in an outside sales role, responsible for project development, which built on the qualifications I had developed in my first position.

When a business owner, building owner or a non-profit organization requested an energy audit from the utility companies, I performed the audit and developed the energy efficiency projects. I also had the authority to develop projects for any "large commercial account" in the greater Boston area, as long as the project qualified for a utility rebate, even if that utility rebate was a custom rebate, whereby I would need to prove justifiable energy savings. A large commercial account simply meant that it was not a residence and consumed a large amount of energy each month.

After performing the energy audits, I was responsible for developing the projects by calculating the energy savings, specifying the equipment and the contractors, quantifying the utility rebates, generating the rebate applications and ultimately selling the projects. I developed projects for many clients and facilities including charter schools, community development centers, senior living communities, churches, cemeteries, high-rise office buildings, pharmaceutical companies, hospitals, parking garages, warehouses, industrial properties, hotels, multi-tenant apartment buildings, full-service exercise facilities, car dealerships, retail stores, restaurants, and bars.

I also developed projects for the Commonwealth of Massachusetts under a statewide energy reduction program that included state department properties such as courtrooms, state parks, mental health facilities, highway rest areas, and public works depots.

While visiting a pharmaceutical company, I found an opportunity to improve interior lighting. Although the company needed more light in their laboratories, I chose to decrease the number of lamps. With this creative and counter-intuitive solution, I was able to increase the lighting levels, eliminate shadows and dark spots, achieve a higher energy savings, reduce the operating and maintenance (O&M) costs, and obtain project approval for a much higher utility rebate.

For a private, international high school, I elected to increase the number of boilers instead of simply replacing the inefficient boilers that existed. Doing so increased control of the building temperature and achieved enormous energy savings (by only running one boiler when it was mild outside). It also reduced their O&M by allowing a cycling of the boilers to operate on specific days. Communicating these benefits to the Board of Directors in Beijing who only spoke Chinese proved to be the hardest part of the project.

A third facility I transformed was an owner managed high-rise office building which had already achieved its annual 5% energy savings goal. The issue was a lack of knowledge about the operation of the building's more than 100 pump and fan motors along with lack of time and resources to investigate.

Instead of developing a project for them, I logged every

piece of HVAC equipment that used a fan or a pump. I provided them with a consolidated list that included the status of the Variable Frequency Drive (VFD) on each. VFD controls the speed of a fan or pump motor, allowing the motor to slow down when conditions allow, thus saving a tremendous amount of energy.

During this time, I worked with roughly 100 clients and developed over $3M worth of projects, interacting daily with my clients, learning their specific challenges, values, and decision making processes.

When I moved from Boston to Austin, TX in 2015, I joined a financial technology company that connected more than 200 energy efficiency providers with financing lenders, allowing the providers to offer multiple repayment options to their clients. As an Energy Project Consultant to the providers, I worked with them throughout their sales cycles, eventually helping evaluate close to $1B worth of proposals.

The providers included large utility companies, multi-national equipment manufacturers, publicly traded energy services companies, property management firms, electrical and mechanical contractors and equipment suppliers.

After a provider (such as a utility company or HVAC contractor) visited a building and found an energy efficiency opportunity, I utilized a large database to benchmark the economics before they sunk hours into project development. By simply providing me with an address and the opportunity type, my experience and background allowed me to provide them with a project cost, energy savings and utility rebate.

In my position, I modified and enhanced providers' proposals. I revised the energy and operations &

maintenance savings (or calculated them if they didn't have the resources to do so), modeled the economics including cash flows, cost of delay, tax incentives, property value increases, and selected the best financing options for the project.

After the proposals were enhanced, I coached and strategized with the providers on presentation tactics and objection handling since they were now proposing a project with a variety of economic benefits and financing options.

I enhanced hundreds of proposals during this time including proposals for lighting, solar photovoltaic, HVAC equipment and energy management systems with annual service agreements.

One of the providers I worked with, a large HVAC contractor, was working with a private university in the Midwest, Quincy University. The school's flagship building, built in the 1800's, had undergone several renovations and expansions throughout the years. The HVAC system was no longer meeting its demands, operating beyond its capacity and useful life. In addition, the school had no capital because they had constructed an athletic facility during the prior year.

An architecture firm had completed an energy audit and submitted it to the school. The university's Chief Financial Officer (CFO) sent it to the HVAC provider, who, at my insistence, referred it to me. My concern was his reliance on the audit to develop a $4M HVAC replacement project. Needless to say, the audit was incomplete and fraught with mistakes.

The energy audit suggested two replacement options. Both the provider and I agreed that the more expensive option was the best solution. This posed the challenge of proving to the CFO that financing the more expensive option was the better economic decision as opposed to phasing the lowest cost option over multiple years. (Phasing is when a project is broken into smaller components and each component is executed as funds allow over time.).

After benchmarking the energy savings for both options, calculating the O&M savings and economic benefits (cost of delay, tax incentives, property value increases), and developing a sales presentation that compared both options side by side, we discussed them with the CFO of the university who accepted our recommendation.

Throughout my career, I've noticed several anomalies that have been consistent regardless of the client, provider, or project type. These include clients with limited time and resources obtaining multiple bids for simple projects, declining "no brainers" and accepting proposals at face value instead of vetting them thoroughly. I've witnessed providers presenting incomplete energy audits and proposals. Some of these are so technical that a client cannot digest them. Others are fraught with mistakes and oversights lacking financial analysis and repayment options. There is also a general lack of buyer's assurance programs in the marketplace and an insufficient amount of industry experts qualified to provide such services.

This led me to found Energy Project Advisors with a vision of providing clients with a trustworthy independent resource to:

1. Objectively screen potential providers
2. Review energy audit reports
3. Grade energy efficiency proposals
4. Recommend wise investment decisions

## *Six Aspects of a Successful Energy Efficiency Project*

Allow me to introduce the six aspects of all successful energy efficiency projects whether obvious or implied. If you're looking at a proposal right now, and any of these six aspects are unclear – WARNING! I would encourage you to take a step back and do your due diligence within the framework this book provides.

If, however, you've been fully briefed on each aspect already, I would still caution you to read this book through to completion. Remember, I'm not trying to sell you on the project. While I would love to assume every salesperson in this industry is honest and sells only high quality projects, I know from experience that is not the reality.

Aspect 1: Alignment with Your Needs

Aspect 2: Qualifications of Provider

Aspect 3: Dependability, Functionality, and Necessity of Equipment

Aspect 4: Savings and Benefits

Aspect 5: Incentives and Tax Credits

Aspect 6: Payment Terms and Options

JEFF JULIA

# CONTENTS

# INTRODUCTION

I'd like you to meet Joe Stevenson, former banker turned restaurant owner. Joe tirelessly strives to maintain and grow his small business since buying a burger restaurant five years ago. He was tired and bored after working 15 years at the local bank, a bank where he had worked since graduating from high school. He decided to take a risk and venture out on his own.

The owner of his favorite burger joint was retiring and wanted to sell. Noticing the boom in local burger franchises, Joe wanted a piece of the action. He struck a good deal with the owner and has since expanded from one location to five across town, despite increasing competition.

Through managing small business accounts at the bank, Joe was all too familiar with the financial consequences of poor construction jobs. Too often, his clients - business owners - would, through no fault of their own, engage in projects to upgrade their facilities or build out new locations, with disastrous results. The flaws embedded in the proposals of these projects led to budget and schedule overruns, installation of low quality equipment, poor workmanship, project management nightmares, unrealistic payment terms, and inclusions of incentives that had long since expired.

Because of this, Joe was very careful to do his homework when undergoing the build-outs of his four newest locations. Now, however, he is faced with the challenge of improving the operation of his original restaurant.

As his day begins, the solicitations start coming in. Sales brochures pile up on his desk. His inbox accumulates faster than he can filter through it. The demands of deliveries, customers and employees are constant. Every interruption blocks him from what he hoped to accomplish. And today he had actually thought he would have a chance to leave early to catch his daughter's softball game!

In navigating through his chaotic day, he spends some time reviewing a repair invoice for his walk-in cooler and scans through the energy efficiency audit in his inbox. He takes a few minutes to digest a quote from an HVAC contractor and deletes the voicemails from countless energy efficiency salespeople who claim they can, "save him some money". In the back of his mind, the same thoughts from yesterday keep replaying:

 Am I going about this the right way?...I don't have time for all this! I need to run a business!...This is not for me...Yikes! I wasn't expecting that number!...I've never heard of that before...This report is too technical..

# ASPECT 1: ALIGNMENT WITH YOUR NEEDS

Since the original restaurant is 20 years old, and no improvements have been made since its grand opening, Joe feels his efforts to improve his business operations should be focused here. Ongoing problems have been hurting his sales and zapping his time.

For the last three months, the kitchen staff has been complaining of excessive smoke generated from the grills during the lunch rush. On several occasions, the smoke has caused the fire alarms to trip, suspending business until the fire department, fire engines and all, have completed their visits. Every time the fire alarms trip, Joe loses $1,500 in fees to the fire department in addition to the loss in customer sales by those vacating the premises and not returning or those who have decided to dine at a safer location.

Two weeks ago, after hearing a radio advertisement during his commute home, Joe called an HVAC company that specializes in replacing air handling equipment. He was told by the receptionist that they would be able to help him resolve the excessive smoke problem. So, Joe scheduled a Project Consultant to visit the restaurant. Last week when the Project Consultant showed up, Joe had to take an hour out of his day to escort the consultant to the roof and around his restaurant. In return, the consultant promised a solution to his smoke problem within a week. The solution has come this morning in the form of a quote attached to an email saying, "Call if you have any questions."

After the Project Consultant visited, Joe listened to a voicemail left by his electric utility company. The automated message stated he might qualify for rebate money. In order to determine if he was eligible, an energy efficiency audit of his business needed to be performed. A toll-free number was given for him to call if interested.

Upon hearing the voicemail, Joe thought, "What the hell? It couldn't hurt." He had called the number and scheduled the audit. He was surprised to learn the audit could be completed within two hours and that there was an opening the next day. However, once again, he would have to take time out to escort the auditor around his restaurant. The results of the audit, he was told, would be emailed to him within 48 hours. Although he'd have to sacrifice a little time, the prospect of receiving money back was alluring enough to follow through with the audit. The results had landed in his inbox in the form of a 10-page report.

Another problem Joe has been dealing with involves his walk-in cooler, where all of his refrigerated product is stored prior to preparation and sale. The cooler has been having difficulty maintaining temperature and completely stopped working this past weekend. The emergency, which cost him $10,000 in spoiled product, added several new headaches. He had to rush order re-supplies of everything in the cooler including meat and produce. Deliveries have been coming in sporadically from several distributors and freight companies. He also had to place an emergency repair call to the service company for an overnight fix so he'd be able to open the store on Monday. As it turns out, that fix was not cheap, costing him $6,500. Between the $10,000 cost in spoiled product, the additional cost of rush ordering re-supplies, and the $6,500 walk-in cooler repair, Joe's emergency funds are exhausted.

With the walk-in cooler problem solved, a quote to fix the excessive smoke problem, and an energy efficiency report in his inbox, Joe decides to take a step back and re-evaluate before spending any more money he doesn't have.

After a long Monday at the restaurant and eating a cold dinner, Joe spends some time with his daughter hearing about her softball game. He then heads into his home office and pulls out last year's financial statements. He compares the statements for each restaurant, line by line, and in doing so, sees an anomaly. The portion of his operating expenses that derive from utility costs at his original restaurant is 45% of his total expenses. The portion at his four newest locations is 30% of his total expenses. Joe figures, if he could reduce his utility costs by 15% at the original restaurant, he would avoid $9,000 in utility expenses each year, be operating at the same efficiency of his four newest locations, and free up some much-needed cash to replenish his emergency reserve fund.

After thinking it over for a few minutes, Joe decides that $9,000 in reduced expenses would be worth it. It would mean the difference between growing his business versus having to close a location. It would mean having the peace of mind that comes with an allocated emergency fund versus living every day with fingers crossed hoping nothing unforeseen happened.

Being careful not to overcommit himself, given his already demanding work load, Joe commits to simply exploring this potential opportunity further over the next few weeks. His livelihood could be at stake if he doesn't.

At first thrilled to find this opportunity, his excitement quickly dissipates. "How the hell am I going to reduce my utility costs by 15%?" he wonders. Thinking about lessons he learned observing business owners while working at the bank, he wants to avoid making similar mistakes when engaging in projects to reduce his utility costs. He understands that energy efficiency retrofit jobs contain unique nuances. He just doesn't know what they are and cannot afford to find out the hard way.

Despite these reluctances, he decides to start at the source of the problem, his electric utility bill. As he pulls out last month's electric bill and begins scanning through it, he notices a line item "Energy Conservation Charge - $.047/kWh". Not understanding what this charge is for, Joe calls the customer service number and connects with a representative named Sally.

Sally tells him that every home and business account pays that fee. It is the source for the energy efficiency rebate (also called "energy efficiency incentive") funds, which are available to all customers performing qualified projects.

Sally continues, "And, because some businesses use so much electricity subsequently paying much more on their Energy Conservation Charges, they have their own account managers."

Beginning to connect the dots, Joe thinks to himself, "Oh, so that is where the rebate money mentioned in the automated voicemail comes from."

Sally re-directs him to the utility's website to learn more.

Joe is now quite excited to dive into the energy efficiency audit report in his inbox. Not knowing what to expect, he considers if it will just be a report stating his current operating efficiency, or, if it will be more action oriented, explaining what improvements can be made and the next steps to take. He wonders if it will show just how much rebate money he can get back. After years of paying the Energy Conservation Charge on his bill, and not knowing where that money went, he is sure he has contributed thousands of dollars to the rebate program. Deciding it best to wait until tomorrow before diving in, he wraps up for the night.

As he lies down for the night, his mind starts wandering to worst case scenarios while he ponders the risks of trimming his utility costs. Knowing he doesn't know much about what makes up the utility cost on his profit & loss statement (P&L), also known as income statement or what the best way to reduce it is, he wonders if the utility company is overcharging him. Maybe they are charging me for multiple meters, or a different business entirely. Dismissing that thought as ludicrous, he is then plagued by the image of his restaurant on fire complete with firemen hosing the burning building as customers and bystanders watch horrified and an electrician apologizes for miswiring a lighting fixture that caused the fire. Trying to shake off that thought, his mind drifts and he sees himself in handcuffs being escorted from a courtroom because a technician working on the HVAC system on his roof fell off and was critically injured. The sub-contractor didn't have enough worker's compensation insurance so the technician sued him. Now he's off to jail, responsible for the horrendous accident.

Coming to his senses, he realizes just how extreme these thoughts are and how remote the likelihood of anything like this happening is. But then reality sets in as he remembers stories from his business clients at the bank. One client lost his business to a worker's compensation lawsuit. Another lost his storefront due to a faulty piece of HVAC equipment catching on fire. A third declared bankruptcy after being stuck with a bill on a construction project that went three times over budget and never solved the problem it was intended to. These thoughts slowly fade as he drifts off to sleep.

The next morning, Joe hardly recalls any of his racing thoughts from the night before and decides to visit the utility company's website to learn more about the Energy Conservation charge as well as the energy efficiency rebates.

Upon arriving at his office, he does just that, and is shocked to see just how many options there are! So many rebate programs are available to businesses like his. So many technologies and types of projects qualify for rebates. There is an extensive list of contractors approved to offer these rebates as well as explanation of jargon and technical white papers available. Feeling awed and optimistic yet overwhelmed and confused, he feels he is on the right track.

He notices there are "New Construction Rebate Programs". Having just finished the most recent build-out, he doesn't recall seeing any mention of these on the proposals he approved! Did the contractors put one over on me? Did I miss out on these funds? Furious, he reaches for the phone to call his general contractor. But just as he does, Joe's train of thought refocuses on the energy efficiency audit report. Keeping his internet browser open, deciding to revisit the issue later, Joe scribbles on a sticky note to "call back GC" and focuses his attention on reading the 10-page audit report.

As Joe reads through the report, he becomes increasingly annoyed at how technical it is, how many terms and abbreviations are used that he is unfamiliar with. Don't these people realize I'm not an energy efficiency expert but a business owner?! On the last page he notices a table, which he can decipher:

## Recommended Improvements

| ECM | Cost ($) | Rebate ($) | Energy Savings ($) | Payback (yrs) | ROI (%) |
|---|---|---|---|---|---|
| Replace rooftop units | $15,000 | $ - | $3,000 | 5 | 20% |
| Install kitchen hood controls | $5,000 | $2,000 | $3,333 | 1 | 111% |
| Install walk-in cooler controls | $2,500 | $1,500 | $1,500 | 1 | 150% |
| Replace Lighting | $7,500 | $2,500 | $1,667 | 3 | 33% |
| Total | $30,000 | $6,000 | $9,500 | 3 | 40% |

40% return on investment!!! Joe is thrilled! He cross-references the table with the utility expense anomaly he found last night of $9,000 per year. If he makes the four recommended improvements, he should exceed that target by $500. Joe couldn't be happier!

Quickly realizing he has no idea what is involved in completing any of these recommended improvements or what they mean, Joe gets nervous and thinks back to his clients at the bank. "Look at where taking risks on construction projects got them," he thinks to himself. "40% ROI is too good to be true. Nothing in the financial world has this good a return without tremendous risk."

In looking at the table, Joe assumes the lowest ROI

improvement of replacing his rooftop units is the least risky and the walk-in cooler controls is the riskiest. He draws this conclusion based on his understanding of the risk/reward idiom in the financial world, where both risk and reward are often correlated.

Joe also recognizes he doesn't have stockpiles of money, particularly $30,000 worth of cash. Even if these improvements all turn out to be low-risk, he'll need some kind of financing vehicle to pay for them. He understands what his options at the bank are – a small business loan or using his line of credit. With low debt and a solid credit rating, he can easily use either. If he is willing to put a down payment of 30%, include a personal guarantee or use an asset as collateral, he knows a small business loan is a viable option. Although this is not ideal, if a quick financial analysis shows it makes sense, he might consider it. But, this would risk putting the efforts of his hard work on the line.

He also knows how high the hurdles are for obtaining a small business loan – down payments, personal guarantees, need for collateral and the amount of paperwork and time required to obtain the loan. He used to process these requests himself when he worked at the bank.

Furthermore, he understands his line of credit should be used for working capital purposes, day-to-day business needs like purchasing new inventory or paying for one-time variable expenses. Joe wonders if there might be a leasing option available, like the one he recently used for his daughter's first car, perhaps through the utility company or a lender that partners with the approved contractors, the energy efficiency providers.

*But I need to be conservative, smart with my money, my livelihood and family depend on it.* He has been conservative though; he hasn't made any changes to his original restaurant and now it's operating at a very low efficiency. He's spending over $9,000 per year, a cost he could be avoiding. Being conservative has cost him headaches and problems, like the one with his walk-in cooler and the smoke issue. These problems are not only taking away his valuable time but his valuable dollars too. In addition, it's costing him business.

He knows that continuing to be "conservative" is going to only increase his inefficiencies and the problems will only compound. Sooner or later, his newest locations will begin to mature and problems of their own will develop. Continued inaction will put his business operations in further jeopardy. His income stream to support his family and his peace of mind will be compromised. His ability to provide others with jobs and support his community will be at risk. Joe weighs the consequences of inaction versus taking action, the calculated risk, and recalls the goal he set last night. He knows in setting his goal, action is required.

If he could afford to be more conservative yet still act on the energy efficiency opportunities that exist, he might start by just considering one improvement that has been tried and true for many years such as replacing his lighting, something he feels somewhat comfortable with. He could start there, see how it goes, and then decide if he wants to pursue the other opportunities once he understands the process and is generating some savings. He could then use these savings to pay for the next improvement.

Thinking a little further, he wonders if the $6,500 emergency repair to his walk-in cooler has been a waste of money. Could they have made the controls improvement instead of the repair and fixed the problem? I could have saved $4,000! Why didn't the contractor tell me this improvement was even an option?

He turns his attention to the HVAC quote in his inbox, the solution to his excessive smoke problem. I wonder if this quote will provide any energy savings or if it includes any kitchen hood controls.

Thoughts racing, Joe takes a break to grab a coffee. As he walks to the coffee shop next door to his restaurant, Joe's mood sours. He begins recalling the experiences of his bank clients. He remembers the consequences of avoidable errors made on their construction jobs: the businesses that closed because the cash flows were unsustainable, the stress, worry and frustration. He recalls the flaws embedded in projects, unbeknownst to his clients, that led to budget and schedule overruns, installation of low quality equipment, poor workmanship, project management nightmares, unrealistic payment terms and inclusions of incentives that had long since expired.

What was the root of all these issues? Were all his clients' victims of the "you don't know what you don't know" dogma? Did they fail to mitigate their risks by cutting corners on their due diligence? Were they reckless, ignorant? Realizing he has been falling victim to the same oversights, the missed rebates on his restaurant build-outs, the misjudgment on his walk-in cooler repair which might have cost him $4,000 extra in unnecessary spending, he ponders how to correct course before moving any further.

What did I do well on the restaurant build-outs? Well, I definitely got customer referrals from the contractors I chose and made sure to call them. I did my research on the equipment they were installing and always considered other alternatives. I mitigated my risks legally and financially, having contracts reviewed by my lawyer, giving myself some wiggle room on budgets, taking advantage of the tax write-offs available for capital improvement projects.

Considering what he's learned since undertaking the build-outs, the new construction utility rebates come to mind. Maybe there are grants available too. In thinking about the HVAC quote and walk-in cooler repair, he realizes that if he doesn't know what he needs, what his options are and specifically how to speak the language of the contractors, he's going to end up with an apple when he really needed an orange.

Joe decides he is going to take a step back and do his investigation to mitigate his risks. With his emergency funds gone, if he is going to reduce his utility expenses by 15%, he can't afford any more mistakes. By committing to simply exploring the opportunity, he has already begun.

Seeing the sticky note he wrote earlier, "call back GC", he decides to leave the HVAC quote in his inbox untouched for the moment and start determining his needs with the general contractor from the build-outs.

The build-outs couldn't have gone better. They were completed under budget, on schedule and without the headaches and disasters his clients at the bank experienced. Despite the gut feeling that he missed out on some monies available from the utility company, which he'll be sure to address, he has no reluctance to do business with the general contractor again, should that prove to be his best option.

In looking at his watch, Tuesday morning has expired, lunch time is quickly approaching. With the cash deficit caused by the walk-in cooler catastrophe, he needs to double down and get his sales up. The phone call will have to wait until tomorrow after his store's special: "Buy a

Premium Burger & Fries, Get a Milkshake Free!" He blocks some time on his calendar to make the call first thing the next morning and begins preparing for the lunch rush with his staff.

# ASPECT 2: PROVIDER

When Joe reaches his desk Wednesday morning shortly after 7AM, he calls the general contractor, Mike McAdams. Joe is surprised to catch Mike at his desk and they spend a few minutes catching up before talking business. Joe informs Mike of the recent developments at his original restaurant: the smoke issue in the kitchen, the walk-in cooler fiasco, and the results from the energy efficiency audit.

"Sounds like you have your hands full, Joe! We might be able to help you out." Mike responds.

He then informs Joe that his contracting business is an approved contractor for the electric utility company, that they install energy efficiency projects all the time. He asks if Joe would be willing to forward him a copy of the energy efficiency audit report so he could review it for him, which Joe gladly does.

"Sometimes these auditors aren't all they say they are, Joe."

"Well, I can tell you one thing, I had to take almost two hours out of my day to escort this guy around and had a hell of a time trying to figure out what his report was saying," Joe replies. "But what do you mean by that Mike?"

"That's just it. These guys don't understand that most people aren't building specialists. They don't understand what this stuff means. You're forced to take time out of your day for a report you can't even make sense of. And, to be a really good auditor, you need to understand a wide variety of building types, energy consuming systems, and energy efficiency improvements. Most auditors are only familiar with a handful, like lighting systems for example. So, in the process of their audit, they miss all kinds of opportunities then send you an incomplete report."

"Funny you say that, Mike. Lighting is one of the four suggested improvements."

After glancing at the report, Mike tells Joe the audit looks good and that they can perform the lighting work in-house. "We have electricians on staff who do these installations all the time". However, he would have to hire sub-contractors, which he will gladly manage, to complete the kitchen hood controls and rooftop unit replacement work. Mike advises Joe that it would be in his best interest if he had the walk-in cooler controls installed himself. "Adding us to that improvement will complicate things and double the cost."

"Let's take a step back, Mike, I'm just trying to figure out if all this work is what I really need. The restaurant hasn't seen an upgrade in 20 years and I'm having some problems that are draining my cash and zapping my time," Joe reiterates.

"It sounds like you're an ideal candidate for some energy efficiency work. There is no shortage of opportunities at your restaurant. You have a sense of urgency but you don't want to put the cart before the horse because your funds are tight. Is that correct, Joe?"

"Yes, that and I've never done any energy efficiency projects before. I mean the build-outs were one thing, but this restaurant is a functioning business. I can't afford to have these impact my operations. I've already spent some money repairing the walk-in cooler, which I'm starting to regret, and I don't want to make any other decisions that I'm going to regret. Before taking the next step, I'm trying to vet this whole thing the best I can."

Mike replies, "That makes good sense, Joe. I'll put together a proposal for the rooftop units, lighting and kitchen hood controls upgrades. Along the way, I'll answer any questions you have. I'm not going to sell you on the work, I'll leave that up to you. I'll simply try to be your advisor."

Jokingly, Joe takes a shot at him, "Is that your newest sales tactic Mike? You're going to be my advisor?"

"Very funny Joe, you're right, we don't make money from it, but you and I both know that most contractors are just going to tell you why you should do their projects. Just like when you leave the car dealership with a 2-door coupe when you really needed a pickup truck."

"Good point, you're right Mike, I appreciate that. I know you guys feed your families from doing projects so I'll keep that in mind."

"You know, these improvements sound almost too good to be true so I just want to understand what all is involved before I make a decision on them. I want to make sure they are in line with my needs and they are the best way to solve my problems."

"Before taking the next step," Joe continues, "who are you planning to use as sub-contractors? And who should I call for the walk-in cooler controls work?".

Mike provides Joe with two companies he plans to use as sub-contractors and one he recommends for the walk-in cooler controls, which Joe writes down on a sticky note.

Being true to his commitment to thoroughly investigate prior to deciding, Joe is going to do his homework on all three, as well as Mike's company. He can't afford any more oversights. He is going to make sure he knows whom he is dealing with and their process before making any commitments.

Joe slips in one last question, "You know Mike, I was on the utility company's website the other day and noticed they have New Construction rebates. I don't recall any of these being included in the build-outs we completed together."

Mike replies, "You're right Joe. That's a good point. Let me have my guys take a look at those jobs. If there was an oversight on our part, we'll discount this project by that amount. Sound fair?"

"Absolutely," Joe responds, "when can I expect your proposal?"

"I'll have to double-check the report you sent over; if it has everything we need, I can get you a proposal next week. Is that okay?"

"Next week is fine, Mike."

After the call, Joe dives into some online research before his staff arrives and the day slips away from him.

He starts by visiting the electric utility company's website, reviewing the list of contractors approved to offer energy efficiency rebates. When looking for the walk-in cooler repair company, he doesn't find their name on the list. "Damn it, these guys aren't qualified! Maybe that's why they didn't bring up the controls option; they didn't want me to go elsewhere. Looks like I'll have to bite the bullet on that one," he thinks to himself.

He also looks for the HVAC company, the one who gave him the quote to replace his rooftop units. Turns out they are not on the list either.

Before deleting their quote from his inbox, he finally opens it. The price he sees makes him laugh. *$25,000! That's almost double the estimate from the energy efficiency audit report.* Knowing he's not only saved a lot of money, but a lot of headaches as well, he happily clicks "delete".

Next, he searches for the companies Mike referenced, as well as Mike's company, just to be safe. He's happy to find all four of them on the approved contractors list. Good start.

After searching the four companies on Google and Angie's List, and reading through numerous reviews and completed projects, he's satisfied. It looks like Mike's referrals have all been in business for a while, have happy clients, and specialize in their respective fields.

Curious to see what he'll find about the HVAC company whose quote he just deleted, he performs the same research. The results are not so glamorous. It looks like they rarely have a happy client. Recognizing a few of the names who wrote negative reviews as his old bank clients, Joe feels as if he has dodged a bullet.

In thinking about working with Mike's company again, he recalls how happy he was with the lighting work of the four restaurant build outs. But he does his research anyway, just to dot his i's and cross his t's.

Feeling satisfied and well accomplished with his efforts, his conversation with Mike, and the fact that he somehow had two hours of undisturbed time, he gets up from his desk at 9AM and turns his attention back to his business.

During the next week, as he awaits Mike's proposal, Joe begins noticing the sheer number of contracting companies doing business in his town. It seems like there is a white van on every street with a different company's name on the side advertising electrical, HVAC, controls, energy, facilities and the like as their specialties. "How can these guys stay in business?" he wonders. "There are so many options!"

He spends some time considering his options from a process and management perspective. Running the restaurant keeps him so busy that he fears taking on any additional management responsibilities, like the energy efficiency improvements, will compromise his core efforts in managing his business.

A business stays in business by making money, he gets that. He also lives by the motto, "You get what you pay for," something his father drilled into his head since he was a kid. Playing devil's advocate, he considers, "Maybe that's not true with energy efficiency companies. I mean, the HVAC company who quoted replacing the rooftop units was priced high and their reviews were horrendous. Were they priced high because they were trying to put one over on me? Or maybe it was because they had some inefficiencies they needed to compensate for: low sales, high labor costs, poor management, lawsuits, high equipment costs. Or could it be that replacing rooftop units wasn't their specialty after all so they padded their margins to be safe?"

These contracting companies are in the business of working on buildings, just like all burger joints are in the business of selling burgers, Joe rationalizes. There are all types of burger restaurants with varying specialties in both product and service. Some restaurants have the most efficient process in the world but the quality of their food is subpar. Others have a great overall restaurant but burgers are only part of their food offering. Some only cater events or offer take-out service. Still others specialize in local, organic ingredients, are very transparent with their sourcing, focusing on burgers only – nothing else. And the pricing, the pricing for these offerings varies widely. Some include bacon and avocado. Others charge extra for each topping and inform you after the fact on the bill. Some new restaurants use pricing discounts to grab a little market share. Others are well known businesses and price does not drive their sales; customers buy for other reasons: customer service, atmosphere, quality, taste and consistency in the product.

Looking at his options in this way gives Joe some clarity and perspective which allows him to put together a list of questions for Mike...questions that will allow Joe to gain some clarity as to how Mike's business operates and how they charge for the energy efficiency project services they provide.

As the week matures, Joe's burger business runs into good fortune. The local paper highlights them as a "Top Local Favorite" over the weekend and, as a result, business picks up dramatically. Relieved that some of the unforeseen costs he's recently experienced will be mitigated with the influx of sales, Joe is feeling a lot lighter when he receives an email, and shortly afterward, a call from Mike mid-afternoon the following Thursday.

"Hi Joe. I have great news for you," Mike starts out. "You were right; those build out jobs should have included $8,000 in New Construction rebates! So here's what we are going to do; we're going to manage these efficiency improvements for you for free. Surprisingly, we had everything we needed in the audit report you sent me, which is extremely rare by the way, to put our price together. That price, discounted by $8,000, is the same total price as the estimate listed in the report - $30,000. For that price, we'll handle all the legwork involved in purchasing the equipment, scheduling the installations, obtaining approval for and payment of the utility rebates, everything will go seamlessly, just like the build outs went. I'm sure you saw my email with the proposal attached. What do you think? Do you have a few minutes to chat?"

"Wow, thanks Mike. That's a lot of information but it all sounds great! Thank you for the discount. I only have a few minutes before my next meeting but I have some questions for you. Over the past few days, I was thinking about these improvements from a process and management perspective, considering my options. I've really got my hands full these days and can't afford any mishaps, any oversights, any cost overruns. And I do not have the time to take on any more management responsibilities. If any of my questions are answered in your proposal, just let me know. I'll review it over the weekend and circle back with you next week."

"Fire away, Joe," replies Mike.

"Ok, I'm sure this is getting ahead of ourselves but when would you be able to start the work and how long will the installations take? I'd like to see if I can overlap the work off-hours with the walk-in cooler controls work so it doesn't impact business operations."

"Right now, Joe, we are about three weeks out on installation. I'll have to coordinate schedules with the sub-contractors and make sure the equipment is available, but we should be able to get the work done over the course of a week and only work mornings so we do not interrupt your business."

"Mike, once you iron that out, will you be able to send me an installation schedule so I can inform my staff and customers?"

"Yes. I'll have a dedicated Project Manager running these jobs for you so there are no hiccups. He will provide you with an installation schedule for your review and approval before we start. If you'd like, we could put up a few signs out front that communicate your energy efficiency initiatives. Some businesses like it as a little free marketing, a differentiator for the eco-minded customer."

"That sounds great, Mike. I'm sure this next one will be spelled out in your proposal but I'd like to ask anyway. Are there any exclusions I should be aware of?...anything that might be line itemed as an extra charge on your final invoice? I don't want any surprises."

"Unlike most of our competition," says Mike, "our price is our price. We don't nickel and dime our customers. Some contractors won't include the cost of recycling the old lighting fixtures or proper disposal of the lamps. Some won't include the cost and responsibility for trash removal. We do."

"Thanks, Mike." Final question before I have to get to my meeting...with new 'controls' for the kitchen hoods and walk-in cooler, I'm guessing that means technology and computers – not my strength. What should I expect? Will you provide training for my staff and me? What should I request from the contractor I'll be managing?"

"We spell this out in the proposal for you. We'll provide a one-year labor warranty. If anything happens within the first year, call me and I'll send a technician over to investigate. We also include a one-hour training for you and your staff on the kitchen hood controls. We've included a brochure of the module we'll be installing for your review; it's an easy-to-understand overview, not too technical. We'll also post the operating instructions next to the module in your kitchen…again, not too technical. There is also a customer support phone number to call on the module itself. Someone who speaks fluent English is available 24-7. There will also be a website listed on the module that has video tutorials and troubleshooting information."

"Sounds good. What about the contractor I'll be managing for the walk-in cooler controls? What should I request from him?"

"For the walk-in cooler controls, you should request everything I just mentioned. Anything less is unacceptable. They are a good company and should have no problem meeting that request. In fact, this should all be spelled out in their proposal, but do yourself a favor and double-check it once you receive it."

After Joe finishes jotting down his notes on a piece of computer paper, he thanks Mike and heads out to meet with his restaurant managers. Today, they are having a round table discussion about improving their payment processing so they can serve more customers more quickly and differentiate themselves from the competition.

On his way to the meeting, Joe calls the walk-in cooler controls company and speaks with the sales manager, Lisa. She informs Joe that she can send a technician out first thing in the morning to gather the information and generate a proposal for him on the spot.

"Really? I've been waiting for a week or two to get a proposal! How are you able to turn it around so quickly?"

Lisa informs Joe that they use the latest technology so their entire process is streamlined. The technicians have laptops and tablets they use to input the information they gather. The software on their devices automatically selects the correct controls package, adds in the cost and the utility rebate, calculates the energy savings and emails the proposal to the customer for approval.

"Wow, that's great," he says as he begins to think about his outdated payment processing system.

Before he hangs up, Joe asks if he should email her the energy efficiency audit report to avoid having the technician visit in the morning. She kindly declines and responds, "With thousands of dollars of your product at stake, we don't make assumptions on these types of projects."

"Good response," Joe replies. "A little inconvenience tomorrow is worth 10 times the headaches I've already experienced with that cooler!

# ASPECT 3: EQUIPMENT – PART 1

On Sunday morning, Joe spends some time in his home office reviewing both Mike's and the walk-in cooler controls proposals, the latter of which was conveniently emailed to him on the spot Friday, while the technician visited. He plans to focus his efforts this morning only on the equipment itself and the manufacturers, breaking the proposals down to bite size chunks.

He wants to be just as careful in vetting the proposals as he was in vetting the companies he selected to provide them. Thinking back, he's glad he did so. Although he had to prioritize it, the potential consequences in time, money and headaches he knows he's avoided are priceless. He shakes his head as he thinks about the HVAC company he avoided doing business with and smiles when considering all he's learned thus far about utility rebates, feeling optimistic about the future, and how his financials might look a year from now. He has set aside his Sunday morning to perform similar research, hoping the few hours in doing so before football starts will also pay off. Then he can relax for a few hours to watch the game.

First, Joe wants to confirm what Mike advised him to double check on the walk-in cooler proposal. After hunting for the information in the proposal for a few minutes, he's happy to see what he hoped to find. Just like Mike had said, the walk-in cooler controls proposal includes a one-year labor warranty, training and technical support information, a brochure of the equipment including installation procedure with a website link for operation and troubleshooting tutorials.

Checking that off his list, Joe next decides to confirm the *quality* of the equipment being proposed. Now that he's comfortable with the providers, are the manufacturers of the equipment of high caliber too? Here, the wheels very quickly start to come off.

He first starts with the lighting section in Mike's proposal, assuming it will be fairly straightforward and easy to understand. After all, they are just lights; how complicated could it be? On the first page, in what appears to be an inventory table of his current lights and what Mike is planning to replace them with, he is already lost.

| Location | Existing Fixture Type | Existing Fixture Description | # of Fixtures | Annual Run Hours | Replace Fixture Type | Replace Fixture Description | Replace Fixture Watt |
|---|---|---|---|---|---|---|---|
| Loading Dock | Metal Halide | MH PS (1) 250W lamp w/LR Ballast | 2 | 4380 | LED | LED Wallpack | 60 |
| Kitchen | T12 | Fluor (4) T -12 ES ISL MAG ballast | 10 | 6880 | LED | LED Tube | 15 |
| Office 1 | T12 | Fluor (4) T -12 ES ISL MAG ballast | 2 | 2026 | LED | LED Tube | 15 |

A bit frustrated and unsure about how he can determine the quality of 1. the manufacturer of the lights without knowing who the manufacturer is and 2. the lights themselves without any product information. He decides to write the questions down in a notebook so he can ask Mike the next day. Before moving on, he notices the "Replace Fixture Watt" column. Knowing the light in the reading lamp on his desk is 65 watts, because he just changed it, Joe wonders how a 15-watt "LED Tube" lamp is going to illuminate his entire office. *Is that a mistake? I wonder what the difference is between the light in my reading lamp and this 15-watt LED Tube lamp. I know the difference between a ¼ pound patty and a ½ pound patty in cost, cooking time, and sales price but not this stuff!"*

Joe skips ahead in Mike's proposal to the rooftop unit replacement section. After reading the executive summary of the improvement with ease, he turns his attention to the equipment:

Model RS020G Nominal 5 Ton VAV Packaged RTU with the following features & accessories to replace Unit RTU-01:

Outdoor, double wall, insulated construction with vertical discharge and return

Variable air volume duct pressure control

0-100% economizer with enthalpy control

(2) 1 HP powered relief direct drive exhaust fans with variable speed motor

Standard low ambient mechanical cooling control

2" MERV 8 filter rack with one set of filter media.

DX cooling coil section with stainless steel drain pan

Laughing to himself, he feels like he needs to know a different language to make sense of this. Why bother listing features and accessories if I can't make sense of them? I have 15 years of experience in banking and Mike expects me to understand all this technical jargon? Should I hire an engineer to make sense of this for me? Maybe the utility company can send somebody out to tutor me so I can make sense of this stuff.

He writes, "translation of entire HVAC equipment section" in his notebook so Mike can explain it all the next day.

In his mind, he sees the phone call getting longer, more complex and begins to worry about how much time he is spending on reviewing everything just to achieve a simple goal.

His mind wanders as he suddenly sees himself five years before, in the same chair in his home office, when he had just bought the burger business. He recalls the countless hours working around the clock, cooped up in his office, eating breakfast, lunch, and dinner in there. It took a toll on him physically and emotionally as well as on his wife and daughter. He remembers just how much he had to learn, how much research and due diligence he had to do. Now he's beginning to feel the same stress, frustration, doubt, and confusion. Joe shakes his head and wonders if there is an easier way to go about all of this. *It would be incredibly helpful if somebody could do this investigative work for me. I need an industry insider who understands the ins and outs of everything involved here. I'd be happy to pay them. It'd be well worth the amount of time I would free up, let alone the emotional baggage I could drop. I'm sure my family would appreciate having me back.*

Taking a quick break to do a Google search, just in case such a resource exists, Joe is disappointed to find no such results. Damn! Hopefully Mike will clear up all this confusion. We did business together before and those projects seemed to turn out okay. Then again, his livelihood depends on the sale.

Without really knowing Mike, Joe understands he is putting a lot of faith in the fact that Mike has his best interests in mind. He's speculating but what other choice does he have? All the data in the world isn't going to give him the trust, understanding, and insight that an industry insider with years of experience would provide. If he wasn't in such a tight spot, he likely wouldn't have started down this path.

As the dialogue in his head continues, he turns his attention back to the kitchen hood controls section of Mike's proposal.

After reading the executive summary, Joe's concerned with the safety of adding controls to his kitchen hoods and doesn't even bother reviewing the equipment itself. He's not a technology expert in the least. If these controls were to fail or go haywire, the safety of his employees, his customers, and his business are at stake.

The kitchen hood's main job, being above the grill, oven, and fryer, is to pull heat and smoke out of the kitchen. How would adding controls improve its ability to do so? Wouldn't that only negatively impact the kitchen environment?

Joe writes down his next question for Mike: explain the operation of kitchen hood controls equipment...safety concerns.

Disappointed with his inability to achieve his original goal of validating the equipment and equipment manufacturers, he turns his attention back to the walk-in cooler controls proposal hoping to have better luck.

When he pulls the proposal up on his computer, he is impressed with the layout and design. A summary, written in layman's terms, of what the installation consists of is front and center. An explanation of the ease of operation rests his nerves for the time being. He is happy to see information about the manufacturer with model numbers as well as a graphic of how the module looks when installed on the cooler itself. Also included is an explanation of each component's role in the system. "Impressive, pretty straightforward," Joe thinks to himself.

As attachments to the proposal, there is a brochure along with specification documents of the equipment. Although Joe does not understand some of the terms and acronyms used, he can understand what components are included and their basic functions: a few sensors, a control box to communicate with his Wi-Fi network and the user interface module itself.

Joe takes the opportunity to visit the manufacturer's website where he finds an informational video explaining the controls system. He searches online for reviews and ratings, just like he did for the contracting companies themselves, and is very happy with what he finds. Discovering a white paper published by the Department of Energy (DOE) on the controls technology, he scans it feeling relieved he's not the only one to have done their homework.

He learns the manufacturer has been in business for over 10 years and specializes only in walk-in cooler controls – nothing else. Their client list is impressive and includes many of the biggest chain restaurants in the country, all noting fabulous results. He learns that the manufacturer trains and certifies local contractors like the one who sent him the proposal so customers have access to ongoing in-person support as needed. He learns that after the installation is complete, the system will operate hands off. If there are any issues, the local certified contractor will automatically receive an alert in real-time and make a visit to the business to resolve the issue before any product is spoiled, 24-hours a day, 7-days a week including holidays.

Satisfied with his findings, Joe feels confident on the walk-in cooler controls improvement but feels very reluctant with the lack of information Mike provided. "Mike is really going to have to convince me the equipment is top notch and worth the investment, not just sell me on the idea of saving some energy," he says to himself.

Stepping back from the proposals, Joe takes some time to consider what other questions he should ask Mike about the manufacturers and equipment. He recalls what was important to him when buying his daughter's new car and, making that comparison, generates the following questions, which he adds to the list already in his notebook:

5. What considerations should I make for a manufacturer? Years in business? Industry focus? Cost? Country of manufacturer? Technology? Government/industry certifications?

6. What should I look for in the equipment itself? Safety? Technology? Age? Performance? Ease of operation and maintenance? Ease of installation?

7. Are the improvements tried and true technologies like gasoline powered vehicles or pioneering technologies like electric vehicles? Are the pioneering technologies safe, risky, expensive?

8. What type of warranty do I want? Full coverage? Or are manufacturer warranties sufficient?

9. How long does the equipment last before I'll need to replace it?

10. What ongoing maintenance is involved with each?

11. Are there efficiency ratings to consider like fuel consumption (MPG) for a car?
12. Are there industry awards to consider like what Motor Trend awards for trucks?
13. Is the equipment delivered to my place of business or to the contractor's place of business?
14. Who is responsible if the wrong model is ordered?
15. What additional options are available and recommended (like navigation system or sun roof for a car)?

If Mike can answer these questions and give Joe the sources he needs to confirm his answers, Joe will feel confident in moving on to review the next aspect of the proposals: the savings and benefits.

As noon approaches, Joe decides it would be nice to take his wife and daughter out to lunch before the football game starts. He shuts down his computer, closes his notebook, stretches, and leaves his office satisfied with the progress he's made this morning.

# ASPECT 3: EQUIPMENT – PART 2

After reaching his desk early Monday morning, feeling light after his team's win yesterday, Joe settles in with coffee in hand and calls Mike.

After reaching Mike, they relive the game before diving into discussing the proposal. Being completely transparent, Joe tells Mike he was trying to validate the manufacturers and equipment but couldn't do so because there was no information.

Failing to reassure Joe of the quality and benefits of the equipment they plan to use, Mike agrees to share the information if Joe agrees he will not bid the job out to other vendors explaining, "We have a big problem with customers bidding out jobs after we've spent a lot of time and resources developing a custom solution for them. They take the proposals, and shop them out for cheaper pricing, often ending up with a subpar solution. I'm not sure if they do it to compare prices, don't understand our proposals, or simply don't trust us at face value but we've had to take steps to protect ourselves."

Joe identifies with all three reasons.

"That makes sense, Mike. I'm sorry to hear that. I just want to make sure you're using high quality products made by companies who have been around a while…manufacturers that offer strong warranties and specialize in these areas: LED lights, rooftop units and kitchen hood controls for restaurants. I don't want a knock-off brand to save a few dollars on the front end. I want a name I can recognize, an industry leader. I'm not asking for the expensive luxury models but I *don't* want the bottom of the barrel. Give me the bang for my buck. If you could send me the brochures of the products you are proposing *and* if I feel confident in what I see, I'll approve them."

Mike understands and tells Joe he'll have to make a few revisions to the lighting before sending the product information to him.

Knowing Joe's funds are constrained, as is the case with most of his customers, Mike takes the opportunity to explain the costs of the improvements.

The two biggest components of the total cost are: 1. the cost of the equipment itself and 2. the cost of the labor required to install it.

If the equipment is expensive but easy to install, the improvement could cost less than an improvement in which the equipment is cheap but very labor intensive to install. "So, changing the lighting products per your request will not change the total cost much because your restaurant is quite small so you don't have many lights and the lights are easy to install, especially on this job, where we are simply replacing the existing lamps and lighting fixtures with new ones."

Mike continues, "If, however, we were redesigning the lighting layout, which would involve removing existing fixtures and installing new ones where none existed, the labor involved would be much higher than the cost of even the best lighting products. The point is, making a few product changes will not impact the cost much *in this particular situation.*"

"For the rooftop units, we are going to replace the existing units with new high efficiency units that will combine perfectly with your existing system. The equipment cost will be a larger component of the total cost because installation only involves disconnecting the old units and reconnecting the new ones in their place. Apart from renting a lift truck to raise the rooftop units from the ground to the roof, labor cost will be a small component of the total cost. You do not need to add an elaborate controls system to the new rooftop units which would dramatically increase the cost because of its labor-intensive nature."

"Mike, why don't I need a controls system for the rooftop units?" Joe asks.

"First off, it is going to be one more thing you'll need to manage. Secondly, it would be very easy for you to change a setting, forget you changed it, and not see any energy savings. Third, you have a small restaurant and a very basic HVAC system. Adding controls is only going to complicate the system, add responsibilities for you, and increase the cost of the improvement dramatically. The rooftop units we are proposing to install have built-in controls for your set-up and, once installed, they will automatically adjust to your thermostat settings, the weather, and the temperature and humidity of the air leaving the restaurant. So, there is no need to add a separate controls system. Let's discuss the manufacturer we are planning to use for these units."

Surprisingly, Joe has heard of the company. In fact, his father used to work there as an engineer. It has been in business for many years and has consistently been recognized as an industry leader in HVAC equipment, winning a variety of industry awards. Mike walks him through each of the features and accessories he is totally confused about, explaining in layman's terms. He informs Joe that some of the features were hand selected for his needs as a restaurant owner. He explains the technology, performance, ease of operation, and maintenance required, as well as efficiency rating, rated lifetimes, warranty, and Joe's remaining questions. Joe ends up approving the equipment over the phone.

He then shifts the conversation to his safety concerns with the kitchen hood controls before Mike begins discussing the manufacturer and equipment quality.

Coming from the banking industry, Joe equates high risk with high reward potential. This risk/reward model would mean both the kitchen hood controls and walk-in cooler improvements are the two riskiest because they have the highest ROI's. He's already disproved this for the walk-in cooler controls concluding the improvement is low risk given the number of fail-safe features he read about. The kitchen hood controls seem far too risky to even consider.

Joe continues, "The kitchen hood's main job, being above the grill, oven and fryer, is to pull heat and smoke out of the kitchen. How would adding controls improve its ability to do so? If these controls were to fail, the safety of my employees, customers and business, would be at stake. This seems too *risky* to cut expenses on, don't you agree?"

Realizing Joe does not understand *why* this improvement is being recommended, *how* the kitchen hood controls function *and* that he is using the risk/reward model from his banking days, Mike addresses his concerns.

## Recommended Improvements

| ECM | Cost ($) | Rebate ($) | Energy Savings ($) | Payback (yrs) | ROI (%) |
|---|---|---|---|---|---|
| Replace rooftop units | $15,000 | $ - | $3,000 | 5 | 20% |
| Install kitchen hood controls | $5,000 | $2,000 | $3,333 | 1 | 111% |
| Install walk-in cooler controls | $2,500 | $1,500 | $1,500 | 1 | 150% |
| Replace Lighting | $7,500 | $2,500 | $1,667 | 3 | 33% |
| Total | $30,000 | $6,000 | $9,500 | 3 | 40% |

First, he educates Joe that ROI is calculated by subtracting the Rebate from the Cost and dividing the difference by the Energy Savings. The *risk* lies within the factors that determine those numbers which include:

the methodology used to develop the Energy Savings (accuracy and assumptions)

achievability of the Energy Savings (equipment quality and ease of operation)

Rebate availability (low risk improvements are often *but not always* correlated with rebate availability)

ease of installation

the supply chain and provider dynamics (which impact cost)

Next, he elaborates on the cause of the smoke issue and why the kitchen hood controls are being recommended as well as how they operate.

"Joe, the reason you are having the smoke issue is because

the fans in the rooftop units cannot remove the amount of smoke you need them to remove anymore. They are old and inefficient. To complicate the matters, the amount of air entering the restaurant (the supply air) is greater than the amount of air leaving the restaurant through the kitchen hood (the exhaust air). This causes a pressure imbalance which in turn causes the smoke to escape the vacuum of the kitchen hood, swirl around your kitchen and trip the fire alarm. Opening your exterior doors when the smoke builds up only complicates the imbalance further. Installing new rooftop units will solve that problem. To offset the cost of the new rooftop units and optimize the only other component of your air handling system, the kitchen hood controls should be installed. Without the kitchen hood controls, it isn't economical to replace the rooftop units. You won't reduce your utility expenses much because the energy savings derive from smoke and temperature sensors that are part of this system. When it is busy at lunch, the fans will provide more air into the restaurant and remove all the heat and smoke from the kitchen hood. When it is slow in the afternoons, the opposite will happen, which is how you will save money without affecting the safety of your staff, customers, or the business itself."

"The system also has a fail-safe mode that turns the fans 100% on, just like they run now. The only preventative maintenance required is somebody on your kitchen staff will need to wipe the sensors off once a week with a wet towel. Otherwise, the energy savings will quickly fail to materialize and the system will operate in fail-safe mode."

Joe is intrigued and reassured by Mike's explanation.

"Also, we will sync the supply and exhaust air so your whole system is balanced. Does that clear everything up for you Joe?"

"Yes. That all makes a lot of sense. Thank you for the thorough explanation. It doesn't sound so risky anymore. Once you share the manufacturer and the equipment model, I'll do a little research just to confirm," continues Joe. "One last question before I let you go… I recall on the restaurant build outs there was a series of tests you guys did once the job was complete. You gave me some documentation of the results and the settings that were configured. What type of start-up and functional testing will you do for these improvements? Will you provide any documentation showing the rooftop units and kitchen hood controls are operating properly?"

Mike proceeds to explain what start-up tests and documentation will be done for each improvement. He also points out the page numbers on the proposal where the start-up and functional testing is clarified.

Joe is pleased to hear this. He knows from experience the consequences of letting this verification step go undone, of assuming the job was done correctly, that no corners were cut.

Joe knows from experience that the crucial test will be after the installation is complete, when everything looks and seems to be working fine, and the final payment has been sent to the provider. He knows if he pays first and inspects later, if he assumes the equipment has been installed properly with no documentation to verify its operation, new costs can accrue rapidly. Sometimes these costs can outweigh not only the financial benefits of the installation, but the non-financial benefits too – like ease of operation and maintenance.

He learned this lesson the hard way after graduating from

high school. The hand-me-down car his parents gifted him had just driven its last mile. With only $2,500 in savings, he had to find a new set of wheels on the cheap. He landed at a local used car dealer recommended by a friend. Upon arriving, he found a car within his budget. The salesman told him everything he wanted to hear so he made the purchase. A week later, when he noticed a significant amount of fluid under the car in his driveway, he returned to dealer. To his disappointment, there was no warranty coverage for the needed repair. As far as the dealer was concerned, it was not his responsibility. Joe felt betrayed and embarrassed. Humbled he examined his role in the situation and how he could have been more thorough.

Before purchasing the vehicle, he had failed to do the proper research on the car dealer. He never even test drove the car or had a mechanic look it over to verify its condition. When presented with the contract, he failed to read the fine print and most importantly he didn't get any documentation listing its condition, or a return agreement should it turn out to be a lemon.

Yes, he was young and naïve but he learned an expensive lesson, one he's always remembered and promised himself never to repeat.

Furthermore, Joe understands he loses all leverage once he pays a contractor the final balance after installation. If a corner was cut during installation, or if a piece of equipment is not functioning as designed, he knows to have it addressed before remitting his final payment.

Joe was purposeful when he withheld final payment on the last restaurant build out. He hadn't received the functional testing certificates. In his eyes, the job wasn't complete and he was right.

Before they hang up, Mike confirms he'll make the lighting adjustments and email him the equipment information later in the day.

As his Monday morning continues, Joe turns his attention back to running his business. Today, he is counting product inventory at the original restaurant. Joe has heard murmurs from his staff that the new manager has been gifting milkshakes to his friends in the evenings before closing the restaurant. So, Joe is making it a point to perform the inventory count himself, a task that is usually the responsibility of the restaurant manager. Obviously, he's going to be very careful when he compares this month's deliveries and sales to inventory in stock for milkshake ingredients.

Later that night, back at his home office, Joe sits down to perform his review of the kitchen hood controls equipment - now that he is comfortable with the operation and safety of the system.

Upon re-opening Mike's proposal and scrolling to the kitchen hood controls section, he is happy to see information about the manufacturer and the equipment model numbers. When he visits the manufacturer's website, Joe notices the layout and design are identical to that of the walk-in cooler controls website. It doesn't take long before he realizes both manufacturers are owned by the same parent company. Performing reviews will be a breeze.

In under 30 minutes, Joe repeats the process he did with the walk-in cooler controls. He reviews the online product brochure, the informational video explaining the operation of the controls system, each component's role in the system, the DOE white paper on the technology, and the reviews of satisfied clients.

Turning to his inbox, it appears Mike was true to his word. An email has arrived containing several attachments. The email proceeds to explain that he included an updated Bill of Materials and cut sheets for every lighting product. He also states, "You'll notice all of the lights are "DLC approved" which means they all qualify for a utility rebate. Don't worry, we'll cross that bridge when you get there in your review."

Relieved he doesn't have to figure out what "DLC approved" means right now, he infers that unless a light is "DLC approved", installing it will not count toward the utility rebate check.

As Joe starts reviewing the Bill of Materials, he quickly recognizes the manufacturer names, all brand names whose lamps he uses in his own home.

Although he doesn't necessarily understand the differences of each type of lamp, he's comfortable enough to move on to reviewing the cut sheets Mike has attached.

Here, he quickly realizes he's going to need more than a basic knowledge of lighting to be able to make sense of them. There are so many terms and acronyms, graphs and tables that he knows he's under qualified to give them the attention they deserve. Taking a few minutes to do an internet search of a few of the terms like "CRI", "lumen output", "wet location" and "color temperature", he learns just how important these factors are.

Another important factor he makes sure he's comfortable with is equipment warranty. From the cut sheets, it appears each light has a full product warranty of five years. Curious what the industry standard is for LED lighting, he does another internet search and is happy to confirm it at five years.

Although he doesn't understand every detail of the lighting cut sheets, he feels comfortable enough having previously executed four restaurants build outs, which included new lighting, with Mike. Mike made the adjustments he requested, he's confident in the brand names and warranties.

Mike also told him on their earlier call that if Joe wanted to install a sample light before completing the full replacement, he'd be happy to do it. And, if he was not satisfied with the light color, fixture, or light levels after installation, he would make any alterations that Joe requested.

Before turning in for the night, Joe sends Mike an email, conditionally approving the specified lights. The conditions are based on Mike honoring his word from earlier that if Joe is unsatisfied with any light post-installation, he'll make the necessary adjustments.

Joe also mentions in the email that he will review the savings and benefits portions of each improvement in the morning and call him with any questions.

# ASPECT 4: SAVINGS AND BENEFITS – PART 1

The next morning, Joe decides to work from his home office. There are no deliveries scheduled, no candidates to interview, no inventory to count, or service contractors scheduled. It is that rare day with nothing particularly pressing that requires his presence at the restaurant, which has hardly ever happened since he went into the burger business five years back.

Before diving into reviewing the proposals, he thinks back to his banking days, generating financial models and risk assessments before lending money to a client. His clients would often submit requests for building improvement projects including credit line extensions, small business loans and mortgage re-financing so they could fund the projects. Joe thinks about how he can leverage this knowledge and perform similar models and assessments to validate the savings and benefits of the energy efficiency improvements he's considering.

The computer models he used at the bank all had built-in assumptions. He would simply input a few variables, based on the client's financial health, and the models would give him the results. He assumes the project consultant from the HVAC company, the auditor from the utility company, and the technician from the walk-in cooler controls company all visited his restaurant for the same reason: to retrieve the variables they needed to put into their models to generate the results he's been shown.

That makes sense but what about the *assumptions* in the models themselves? What are they? If the basic assumptions are not accurate to his specific operation, how much are the resulting savings and benefits affected? Who makes the models that are used? Who certifies them? Are they just some spreadsheets a junior engineer created or are they industry accepted software programs? What is the methodology behind them?

Joe jots down the questions for Mike in his notebook. The models he used at the bank also compared the financial health of his clients to the health of similar clients in the database. This comparison allowed Joe to see where the client was in the full range profiles. From this information, Joe could gauge whether the client's request would be approved based on the data for comparable clients, enabling him to avoid many hours of processing requests that would ultimately be denied.

Making a comparison with the four improvements he is considering, Joe thinks it would be helpful to see the full range of costs, rebates, and savings for restaurants like his in Mike's database. He writes down another question for Mike, "Where do these improvements rank in your database for restaurants like mine?"

Continuing to brainstorm, he considers if the energy savings (the avoided utility expense) is only one piece of the savings and benefits pie. This piece, which appears to be in line with his utility cost reduction target of $9,000, looks good, but what other savings and benefits are there? What non-financial benefits are there? Which of these does he care about?

The answer is his values. Obviously, the comfort and safety of his staff and customers are important, but he also values his time and emotional well-being…making it to his daughter's softball games, having the time to take his family out to dinner. These values have somehow been compromised recently. Jotting down some thoughts he writes:

- More time to spend with wife and daughter: softball games and dinners
- Better comfort in kitchen and dining area; kitchen is hot & dining area cold
- No additional time commitments required to operate and maintain the new equipment
- Brighter exterior lighting for safety and to attract customers
- Less dark spots inside restaurant to improve presentation of food
- Advertising to attract eco-minded customers
- Less risk of losing products in walk-in cooler
- No more emergency repairs
- No more fire alarms tripped in the kitchen
- Higher property value
- Ability to write-off new improvements on tax return and depreciate costs

These, he concludes, are really *why* he is spending so much time and focus on improvements: to make sure he obtains the benefits he values most. Otherwise, the improvements are good from a financial perspective because they save his business money on utility expenses, avoiding further losses, but not worth his overall investment of time and mental energy.

Realizing it is all about values, he commits to determining if the energy efficiency improvements will achieve all of what is most important to him. If he can't find mention of these benefits when he reviews the proposals, he will ask Mike for his expert opinion, which by now, he is beginning to trust. If Mike cannot confirm the realization of these benefits, he'll really have to consider whether this is the best course of action.

Joe begins to probe a little deeper. He knows the equipment will improve the value of the building, which he owns. With the higher building valuation comes an additional tax burden. Thinking back to the build outs, he recalls a meeting he had at the end of the year with his accountant. He remembers one financial benefit of installing new HVAC equipment was the ability to depreciate the cost over its useful life. He wonders if he can use this "cost segregation" technique for the new rooftop unit improvement, either for the units being removed or the new ones. He wonders if there are any limited time tax policies he can take advantage of for installing energy efficient equipment.

Joe decides to send his accountant an email explaining the improvements he's reviewing to invite his input on the tax side. He wants to be safe but at the same time leverage policies already in place. Joe hasn't been in the financial industry for a few years now and knows the policies change regularly. Policies on depreciating capital equipment, tax write-offs for financed equipment, and limited time deductions are not static.

Just like the energy efficiency rebate policies offered by the utility companies, tax policies also change continually. These tax policies are created to encourage businesses to make investments in energy efficiency upgrades by making them financially attractive even if a business is in a region where the utility companies do not offer rebate programs.

During his time at the bank, some of his clients took advantage of the tax and accounting policies that existed for new construction projects, renovations, and capital equipment purchases. He's also heard stories of not so savvy business owners getting too aggressive with those options, not consulting their accountants, and winding up in legal trouble.

Turning back to the list of benefits he jotted down, he takes a moment to consider the possibilities around sustainable advertising. Joe has had trouble reaching the more environmentally conscious customers and is often asked whether his produce is local and organic or if his beef is grass-fed. He does offer recycling at his restaurants and has been considering changing his purchasing model but wonders if these energy efficiency improvements can be utilized in a marketing sense. Open to creative ideas, he sends an email out to his restaurant managers asking for input.

Shifting his focus to the proposals, Joe decides to start by evaluating the savings and benefits of each improvement individually, then the four improvements as a whole.

He begins by performing some calculations of basic ratios, the same way he started evaluating requests from his bank clients. Not knowing which considerations should be made, he decides to determine what the "savings to cost and savings + rebate to cost ratios reveal. He doesn't know if these are important ratios to evaluate or where on the spectrum the results fall, so he writes down another question for Mike to answer, "Which calculations should be performed to evaluate the cost to benefits and what results are considered good?" His calculations result in the following table.

| ECM | Cost ($) | Rebate ($) | Energy Saving ($) | Savings Cost (%) | Savings +Rebate/ Cost (%) |
|---|---|---|---|---|---|
| Replace rooftop units | $15,000 | $ - | $3,000 | 20% | 20% |
| Install kitchen hood controls | $5,000 | $2,000 | $3,333 | 67% | 107% |
| Install walk-in cooler controls | $2,500 | $1,500 | $1,500 | 60% | 120% |
| Replace Lighting | $7,500 | $2,500 | $1,667 | 22% | 56% |
| Total | $30,000 | $6,000 | $9,500 | 42% | 76% |

From his perspective, Joe concludes the savings to cost result for the whole project of 42% is really good. It means for every dollar he spends, he'll receive $0.42 back in energy savings for the life of the equipment. When he includes the rebates, the $0.42 then becomes $0.76 for every dollar he spends. Figures like this in the banking world are unheard of. Investments almost never yield results like this.

Looking at the Energy Savings Total of $9,500, Joe divides by 12 to see what the improvements could save him monthly, or in other words, how much he loses for each month he delays his decision.

"$792! Wow!" Joe thinks to himself. "Our best-selling lunch special is priced at $7.99, which means every month, the revenue produced by selling 100 of these lunch specials is squandered on our energy inefficiencies. I could be doing a lot with that revenue! That's heartbreaking to see. Clearly our energy intensity is killing our profitability."

Already satisfied with the ROI and payback figures presented for the improvements, he recalls the equipment life from a conversation with Mike during the build outs. Mike mentioned the average equipment life of rooftop units is 20 years. LED lighting is about 10 years (if they are not on 24/7). The same is true for controls systems.

Joe decides to calculate the total energy savings for each of the four improvements using these equipment lifetimes, curious how the ROI's will improve. His calculations result in the following table.

| ECM | Cost ($) | Rebate ($) | Equipment Life (yrs) | Annual Energy Savings ($) | Total Energy Savings ($) | ROI (%) |
|---|---|---|---|---|---|---|
| Replace rooftop units | $15,000 | $ - | 20 | $3,000 | $60,000 | 300% |
| Install kitchen hood controls | $5,000 | $2,000 | 10 | $3,333 | $33,333 | 607% |
| Install walk-in cooler controls | $2,500 | $1,500 | 10 | $1,500 | $15, 000 | 560% |
| Replace Lighting | $7,500 | $2,500 | 10 | $1,667 | $16, 670 | 156% |
| Total | $30,000 | $6,000 | | $9, 500 | $125,003 | 406% |

"406% ROI! Total avoided energy cost of $125,003! Those can't be right; there's no way," Joe says to himself.

He carefully reviews his calculation and confirms the

results. Over the useful life of the equipment for each improvement, the return on his investment of $30,000 will be 406%. With returns like this he wonders, "What's the catch? What am I not seeing? This is way too good to be true. There must be a 'got ya' somewhere."

Knowing the Total Energy Savings is based on the units of energy that will be saved multiplied by the utility rate (cost per unit of energy the utility company charges), he wonders if the "got ya" lies in an over estimation of the utility rate.

"Perhaps this is one of those assumptions made in the financial models causing these unbelievable returns," he questions.

Scanning through Mike's proposal, he finds the utility rate used, $.14/kWh and cross-checks it with his actual utility bill. Turning to the most recent electric utility bill he received, Joe divides the total charge by the kWh (unit of energy) the restaurant used and gets $.14/kWh. They match.

"Hmmm, interesting."

Accurate, but not revealing the answer he's looking for, he thinks further. "I know my bill has been going up every year since I bought the business. I also know the utility rate has increased by 4% every year because of the local news stories on increasing energy costs. Maybe *that* consideration wasn't factored into Mike's calculations. But, even if it wasn't, including it would only improve the return on investment."

Stumped, Joe thinks that perhaps when he reviews the fine print, the terms and conditions, he might find a sentence buried in there that explains the catch. For now, he'll continue with his due diligence, cautiously optimistic.

"No more emergency repairs" is a benefit he values and he knows he can quantify it simply by totaling his receipts.

Over the past year, Joe has kept records of invoices and receipts for maintenance and repair costs. Opening the folder in his desk where he's stored these, Joe adds them up. When he includes the costs of tripping the fire alarms, repairs to the HVAC, replacement lamps, the walk-in cooler fiasco, he gets a big number: $11,375.

Initially, when he first saw the energy efficiency audit report, he was just glad to see the total energy savings align with his $9,000 utility expense reduction target. But now, as he digs deeper, quantifying the financial benefits he values, which have been left out of the proposal, he realizes the $9,000 annual energy savings was just the tip of the iceberg. In addition, he hasn't even spoken to Mike yet about the non-financial benefits he values.

Seeing an email come in from one of his restaurant managers replying to the eco-advertising email he sent, Joe opens it. The suggestion the manager makes is for an advertising campaign that communicates the "offset in carbon emissions from the atmosphere from performing the improvements." The manager continues, "We could have a banner made to hang from the storefront with a message like, 'Our upgrades just took 'X' cars off the road,' or 'We just planted 'Y' trees in our restaurant with new LED lights." The manager reasons, "Some of our customers care about reducing their carbon footprints and supporting businesses that share the same values."

Knowing this is an important opportunity to capitalize on, Mike would need Joe to provide him with those carbon emission savings first so he can communicate the energy efficiency initiatives to the community and attract new eco-minded customers.

Entertained and optimistic about the possibilities, Joe jots down in his notes for Mike, "how many carbon emissions will the improvements offset?"

Another email comes in from his accountant. His accountant confirms that there are specific benefits which he could help with at year end and advises Joe to keep a record of the costs of the improvements, the make and model numbers of the HVAC units being removed as well as a simple log of the lights that will be replaced. He also provides Joe with a link to a tax incentive called Section 179D, which he'd be happy to explain. Reassured, he emails a thank you.

In need of answers to his questions which are piling up, Joe calls Mike shortly before 9AM. Disappointed to reach his voicemail, he hangs up and decides to send Mike an email instead. In the email, Joe lists the questions he would appreciate answers to and notes that he would like to discuss several non-financial benefits that are of utmost value to him.

With the email sent and his cell phone ringer on, Joe wraps up his savings and benefits due diligence at home, grabs a few snacks, and heads over to the restaurant to support his team prepare for the lunch rush.

# ASPECT 4: SAVINGS AND BENEFITS – PART 2

On his way home that evening, Mike calls. "Hi Joe, I saw your email and have some time now if you'd like to talk through your questions."

Joe starts by asking Mike about the energy savings models, particularly the assumptions used and methodology. He wants to determine if the financial benefits, and energy savings, are accurate.

Mike informs Joe of the bad news first. "There are no government regulated software models for calculating energy savings. Every provider does not use the same program. There are three basic methodologies.

The first is calculated energy savings. Every company in the energy efficiency business that performs these calculations either uses proprietary software or a spreadsheet they've developed as their methodology. They are all based on the laws of science. Some providers make more of an effort than others to achieve accuracy in their assumptions. I'll discuss with you momentarily what those are.

The second is a benchmark or database methodology. This is simply a comparison of your restaurant to other similar restaurants in the provider's database.

The third is an estimated energy savings methodology. The

energy savings are provided by the utility company and known as the deemed savings. These are pre-determined estimates that the utility company recognizes for each improvement, which they leverage for the rebate programs they offer. The how and why would require a separate conversation.

Because these methodologies generate estimates rather than absolute guarantees, providers use a disclaimer stating the energy savings in the proposals are estimates not guarantees.

However, there are industry accepted Technical Reference Manuals which lay out the equations and variables needed to calculate energy savings for a wide variety of energy efficiency improvements. We use those manuals to develop our spreadsheets and make sure we limit the number of assumptions by insisting that a site visit is made for every proposal we develop. The auditor from the utility company who put together the energy efficiency audit report for you saved us this step by making a visit of his own. He was very detailed and allowed us to confirm all of the assumptions with the accurate data he obtained from your restaurant for all three improvements in our proposal."

Joe replies, "What assumptions are you referring to? Can you give me some examples, say for lighting?"

"Sure, Joe. For lighting, there are several assumptions. Most of the existing light fixtures in your restaurant use fluorescent lamps. There is something called a *ballast* which regulates the electric current to the lamps. Every fluorescent lighting fixture has one. There are several types of ballasts and some of them are considered hazardous waste because they contain PCBs. The auditor who visited your restaurant had a handheld tool which allowed him to determine which type of ballast powered each fixture. If a site visit had not occurred or he had not used the handheld tool, several consequences could have resulted. For starters, the energy savings could be inaccurate as some ballasts consume more energy than others. Although you only have a small quantity of lights in your restaurant, imagine the impact of a slight error in this assumption in a large hospital with thousands of lighting fixtures. Second, disposal costs for ballasts with PCB's is significantly more expensive because they are hazardous waste. Imagine being told by the electrician, once the project is underway, that an oversight has been found and that this oversight requires the approval of a Change Order of several thousand dollars to dispose of the ballasts properly."

"Although these cases are rare, they do occur. One assumption that is *very commonly inaccurate* is the annual run hours, which is the estimated amount of time the lighting fixtures are powered on over the course of the year. If, in the energy savings model, this assumption is inaccurate, the impacts of the savings are dramatic. Sometimes, contractors manipulate this variable to match a financial metric like payback or ROI which the customer stated up front he needed before they could approve the improvement."

"That's terrible! How dishonest," Joe responds.

"Unfortunately it does happen and is rarely detected. But don't worry, Joe. I'll explain how we determine accurate annual run hours for you on this improvement. Do you have our proposal in front of you?"

Joe states that he does.

"If you scroll to the lighting section in the proposal, on the first page you'll notice an inventory table of your current lights and what we are planning to replace them with."

Joe recalls this table from Sunday morning. This is the table that confused him.

| Location | Existing Fixture Type | Existing Fixture Desc. | # Of Fixtures | Annual Run Hours | Replace Fixture Type | Replace Fixture Description | Replace Fixture Watt |
|---|---|---|---|---|---|---|---|
| Loading Dock | Metal Halide | MH PS (1 250 W lamp w/LR Ballast | 2 | 4380 | LED | LED Wallpack | 60 |
| Kitchen | 112 | Fluor (4)T12-ES ISL MAG ballast | 10 | 6880 | LED | LED Tube | 15 |
| Office 1 | 112 | Fluort (4)T12-ES ISL MAG ballast | 2 | 2026 | LED | LED Tube | 15 |

"You'll notice a column titled Annual Run Hours. When the auditor from the utility company visited you to perform the audit, did he ask you questions like, "What are your store hours? What time do you start preparing food in the kitchen? What time does the first staff member arrive? Do you turn the lights off when you leave each night?"

Joe recalls a peppering of questions just like these by the auditor and replies, "Yes, he asked me all of those and more."

"Good," Mike says. "What he was doing was determining the Annual Run Hours for each area of your restaurant based on your responses. The more information you provided, the more precise he could estimate them and thus, the more accurate the energy savings will be once the new lights are installed. Another way he could have determined the Annual Run Hours is by placing data loggers throughout your restaurant which automatically determine when the lights are on and when they are off. Two site visits would have been required and this tactic is typically used in very large buildings where making accurate assumptions are very difficult. Examples would be a college dorm room or the offices in a research laboratory building."

"Does that all make sense Joe?"

"Yes it does. This is helpful insight," Joe says.

"Good. Now would be a good time to elaborate on my email mentioning that all the lights are DLC approved."

"I was hoping you'd bring that up, why is DLC approval important?" asks Joe.

"DLC stands for DesignLight Consortium, a non-profit that promotes high quality energy efficient lighting products. Lighting manufacturers voluntarily submit their products to DLC for quality testing. The products that pass the tests are listed on DLC's Qualified Products List, known as the 'QPL'. Unless a lighting product is DLC approved, meaning it's on the QPL, it typically does not qualify for a utility rebate. Utility companies rely on the DLC QPL as an independent checks and balances so rebate money is not squandered on improvements that use low quality lighting products and fail to achieve energy savings."

"Thanks for the explanation! That is definitely an important benefit for us," Joe replies. "Switching gears a bit, Mike, where do the three improvements rank in your database? I'm trying to make a comparison here to other proposals you've developed. Are these in the top 10%, the middle, or the bottom 10%?"

Mike answers, "All three of these improvements are in the top 10%. They are all A+ opportunities. The ROI is through the roof as I'm sure you already know. It seems almost too good to be true, I know but the reason the financial benefits are so high is because your current setup is so energy intensive. No improvements have been made for 20 years which is almost unheard of. Imagine evaluating the efficiency of a 20-year-old car versus the efficiency of a brand-new hybrid or electric vehicle. So much has improved in the past 20 years that the efficiency difference is astonishing!"

Joe knows Mike is right. It sounds like there might not be a, "got ya" after all.

Mike continues, explaining to Joe some industry-wide ballpark expectations for each of the four improvements: "Rooftop unit replacements typically have paybacks at about the 10-year point. It's difficult to obtain utility rebates especially if the units are at the end of their useful life of 20 years.

Kitchen hood controls usually pay back in less than five years. If the existing kitchen hood fans run at full speed around the clock, the paybacks are in less than two years. Between the savings and rebates, these improvements almost always make sense in a commercial kitchen.

The walk-in cooler controls have even better paybacks, almost always under two years. They are cost-effective, quick, and easy.

Lighting paybacks vary dramatically but are almost always under 10 years, and in most cases, under five years.

Remember though, there are variables unique to every situation and payback is a matter of cost/savings, but these are good benchmark figures."

Joe responds, "Interesting. Sounds like you know your stuff! The numbers looked too good to me too so I ran a few calculations of my own to try to bridge the gap from my banking experience to these energy efficiency improvements. I calculated the savings to cost and savings and rebate to cost ratios. Which calculations should I be performing to evaluate the cost to benefits. What results are typical?"

"Well, Joe, you are asking all of the right questions which is great to hear. Besides payback and ROI which we provided for you, the ones I would suggest are savings to cost ratio, like you've performed, as well as total lifecycle savings which you calculate by multiplying the Annual Energy Savings by the equipment lifetime. That is usually a huge number that convinces customers the improvements are very valuable. Cost of delay is important too. Take the Annual Energy Savings and divide it by 12 months. That way you can see how much money you are losing by delaying in moving forward with the improvements every month. You can also look through your book of receipts and calculate the total avoided loss in repair and maintenance costs by performing the improvements. All of those are good convincers."

Feeling ahead of the game, Joe smiles knowing he's already calculated these and saw unbelievable results. He thanks Mike for confirming his calculations and decides it's time to switch gears to discuss the remaining non-financial benefits he's identified as most valuable to him:

- Better comfort in kitchen and dining area: kitchen is hot

    & dining area cold
- no additional time commitments required to operate and maintain equipment
- brighter exterior lighting for safety and to attract customers
- less dark spots inside restaurant to improve presentation of food

As the two go through each one, Mike confirms that Joe will realize these because of the improvements and explains exactly how, reiterating some of the points they've already discussed.

With Mike's confirmation, Joe fires off one last question before ending the conversation. Explaining to Mike the advertising idea of his restaurant manager to attract eco-minded customers, he asks, "How many carbon emissions will the improvements offset?"

Mike informs him he has the number in his software program and will gladly email it to him. He explains the unit of measure for carbon emissions is "metric tons." To visualize one metric ton of carbon emissions, he tells Joe to imagine a 27ft x 27ft x 27ft cube.

Thinking to himself that he now has what he needs to continue with his review efforts *and* a great idea for an advertisement, Joe thanks Mike and ends the call.

Taking a few notes from the conversation and scanning the proposals for what to review next, Joe realizes that he has not yet investigated the utility rebates. Based on what his accountant stated in his email, there appear to be some tax incentives to investigate as well.

Joe figures the utility rebates and tax incentives are the next logical piece to review. Before ending work for the day, he sends an email to his accountant scheduling a phone call.

# ASPECT 5: INCENTIVES AND TAX CREDITS - PART 1

Joe wakes up to a cold and rainy Wednesday morning. Exhausted from back to back 12-hour work days, he feels an immense urge to just pull the covers over his head and hit snooze. Entertaining this thought a little bit he wonders if he is demanding too much of himself. Maybe he should just agree to the improvements, sign the proposals and move forward without further exhausting himself with research. *Mike is the energy efficiency expert. After all, I'm a business owner with a family that does not see me nearly enough.*

Suddenly, he remembers the costly fiasco with his walk-in cooler and the fact that his emergency funds are depleted. With a rush of adrenaline, he knows he must keep going. Lying in bed isn't going to get my bank account healthy again. And not completing what I started is just going to lead to more headaches down the road, I've already proven that to myself.

After washing up and settling into his home office with his coffee in hand, Joe checks his email. His accountant has responded and is available before 9AM for a phone call to discuss the current tax incentives available for energy efficiency improvements.

Joe picks up the phone, calls Phillip, his accountant, and begins his tax questioning.

Phillip gives an overview explaining that if Joe finances the work, he can write off the interest.

"For the equipment that is removed," he says, "we can depreciate the remaining value up to certain limits. And for the new equipment that is installed, some of it might qualify for accelerated depreciation, also known as MACRS. You can learn more about this at www.energy.gov."

He then explains the third option, known as the EPAct Section 179D tax deduction. "For both MACRS and 179D, we partner with a third-party firm which will work with you directly to process the paperwork and provide the final numbers for your tax returns. As with processing a utility rebate, this third-party firm will handle everything. The first step would be to connect you with them as soon as you decide to perform the improvements."

Joe wonders if it's worth adding another company to the mix and if the benefits of leveraging these options are worth the hassle so he asks what kind of tax savings Phillip is talking about. Is it worth the effort?

"You mentioned two of the improvements are lighting and HVAC upgrades, right?" Phillip asks.

"Yes, both."

"Then, yes. They are worth it. Plus, there is no additional burden to you. All you have to do is provide our partner with a few numbers and sign a few documents and they handle the rest. And the kind of tax savings you can expect are significant. We can deduct all of the interest payments, 2% percent of both the lighting and HVAC improvement costs every year with MACRS and up to $1.80/square foot with the 179D deduction."

Taking notes, Joe realizes that although he hasn't reviewed the rebates on Mike's proposal yet, he doesn't recall seeing any mention of "MACRS" or "179D".

"Sounds good," says Joe. "I'll take your advice on this. I don't recall seeing any mention of tax rebates or incentives on the proposals. Is that a common oversight from your experience or does that mean the improvements we're considering do not qualify for them?"

Philip explains, "There is hardly ever any mention of these tax policies on energy efficiency proposals. They change regularly. Most providers do not understand them and see them as a risk rather than a benefit to their clients. We make it a point when we begin the tax filing process, to ask all our business clients if they had any work done to their facilities over the past year. Sometimes, it's not too late to leverage these tax policies for them. If you do decide to move forward with the improvements, I can connect you to our partner who will handle everything so I can make the adjustments on your tax return."

After ending the call with Phillip, Joe performs a quick back-of-the-hand calculation to see how significant the tax savings might be...a ballpark number. He estimates an interest rate of 9%, a rate he recently got for a small personal loan. Using an Excel formula, he gets a first-year interest total of $4,500 on a loan of $30,000. He adds that $4,500 to 2% of the combined lighting and HVAC cost ($450) to get $4,950.

Joe knows his restaurant is about 2,500 square feet. Multiplying that by $1.80/square foot and adding this subtotal to the $4,950, Joe obtains $9,450.

"Phillip wasn't kidding when he said the tax savings would be significant," he says to himself. At almost $10,000, the tax savings are nearly 30% of the total cost of the improvements, *before* taking the utility rebates into account!

Having already forgotten about the resistance he had before the call, Joe takes out the energy efficiency audit report and begins reading through the language on utility rebates.

He understands how the rebate funds are generated, from a small charge on everybody's utility bill, but he doesn't understand exactly why this charge and the rebate programs exist in the first place. Is it just to generate economic activity? Are utility companies required by law to reduce each customer's energy consumption? It doesn't make sense. Utility companies make money from the amount of energy used by their customers. The more energy used, the more money they collect as revenue. So why incentivize customers to use less energy if that means getting paid less?

"Good questions to ask the utility company," he thinks as he writes them down.

On the last page of the energy efficiency audit report, he refreshes his memory with the rebates for each of the four improvements.

improvements.

## Recommended Improvements

| ECM | Cost ($) | Rebate ($) | Energy Savings ($) | Payback (yrs) | ROI (%) |
|---|---|---|---|---|---|
| Replace rooftop units | $15,000 | $ - | $3,000 | 5 | 20% |
| Install kitchen hood controls | $5,000 | $2,000 | $3,333 | 1 | 111% |
| Install walk-in cooler/freezer controls | $2,500 | $1,500 | $1,500 | 1 | 150% |
| Replace Lighting | $7,500 | $2,500 | $1,667 | 3 | 33% |
| Total | $30,000 | $6,000 | $9,500 | 3 | 40% |

Joe remembers Mike saying there are no rebates for replacing the rooftop units because, "they are at the end of their useful life," and wonders why. "Wouldn't the utility company want me to replace them if they are old and inefficient? I mean they *are* offering rebates to be more efficient, right?" he asks himself, as he writes down another question for the utility company.

"Wait a minute, when I first reviewed this report, I called customer service. The representative I spoke with told me some accounts have their own account managers," Joe says to himself. "Maybe I'm one of them and my account manager can explain to me why there is no rebate for the rooftop unit replacement and why the rebate programs exist in the first place."

Deciding the best use of his time is to get clarification on this before he goes any deeper, Joe calls back customer service. After navigating through the automated response menu, he connects with Mary, a customer service representative for the commercial energy efficiency rebate programs.

Joe explains to Mary his current situation, that he is reviewing two proposals, four energy efficiency improvements total, and has some questions about the rebate programs. He starts by asking her why the rebate programs exist in the first place?

Mary responds, informing Joe that the rebate programs exist for a few reasons. "It is more cost-effective for the utility company to incentivize customers to reduce their energy consumption than it is for them to increase the capacity of the grid infrastructure itself and buy more energy from the generation sources (the power plants, wind farms and solar fields). Also, there are government programs and regulations utility companies need to comply with that reward energy reduction. If you'd like to learn more, you can visit the Department of Energy's website at www.energy.gov or the Federal Energy Regulatory Commission's website at www.ferc.gov."

Joe asks, "My contractor told me there are no rebates for replacing the rooftop units because they are 20 years old and at the end of their useful life. Why is that?"

Mary proceeds to explain the difference between elective and required improvements. "Elective improvements are the ones that businesses wouldn't otherwise be incentivized to perform if there were no rebate programs. If the numbers didn't look attractive on the proposals and their existing equipment was working fine, upgrading it would be a low priority, like LED lighting for example.

If the rooftop units stopped working and you had no heating or air-conditioning for your restaurant, you would have to replace them anyway. So, by offering a rebate for that improvement, we would be giving away rebate funds that could have gone toward incentivizing an elective upgrade. That is why we don't offer a rebate for replacing equipment at the end of its useful life."

Not the answer he was hoping for but it makes sense.

Joe informs Mary that the last customer service representative he spoke with said that some businesses have their own dedicated account managers and asks if he might be one of them.

Mary asks Joe for the account number on his utility bill and pulls up his information in her system. "Unfortunately, it looks like you do not have an account manager. I see five locations here in our system. You own several restaurants, correct?"

"Yes. Why am I not assigned an account manager? What determines who gets one and who doesn't?"

Mary replies, "All utility companies have different structures but here, we only dedicate account managers to the largest 10% of our commercial and industrial accounts. These accounts consume the most energy and have the highest kW demand which, if unmanaged, really strains the electric grid. These accounts are typically large manufacturing facilities, hospitals, colleges, distribution warehouses and data centers. Restaurants and small brick and mortar retail businesses have a very small kW demand in comparison. So, we have the customer service team, our online resources and the approved contractors to support small accounts like yours."

Again, not the answer he was hoping for, but he thanks her anyway for the explanation.

Joe proceeds to inform Mary of the amount of work he's had to do up to this point: screening the providers, validating the equipment, confirming the savings and benefits, learning about the tax incentives, and now trying to understand the utility rebates. He notes the sheer number of hours he's spent researching, phone calling, and escorting visitors to his restaurant. He's exhausted and disappointed it's up to him to figure this all out. Curious to find out if there is a better way, a resource available that could do this for him, he asks Mary.

Her response surprises him. "There is a business that performs this service for businesses like yours. They are an independent firm, not affiliated with any of the providers or manufacturers. They are a small team of industry experts familiar with all facets of energy efficiency projects. They have experience calculating engineering savings, developing proposals, managing installations, confirming rebates, performing financial modeling and vetting the payment terms and financing options. If you send them a proposal, they can perform all the due diligence on your behalf. They make it easy and boil everything down into a report card, which they discuss with you, to educate and advise you of their findings. Their fees are well worth the value they provide.

(Spoiler alert, Energy Project Advisors is the company she's referring to.)

Joe replies, "At this point, I would pay almost anything to have this done for me."

"Joe, what is your email address? I'd be happy to send you their contact information."

After giving Mary his email address, Joe asks how the rebate amounts are determined. "Are they fixed rebate amounts or do they vary based on factors like the amount of energy the improvement will save? What is the process to receive the rebate check?"

Mary informs him that all this information is available on their website and the Database of State Incentives for Renewables & Efficiency's website, http://www.dsireusa.org/. But, she'll do him a favor and explain it now.

Mary tells Joe there are two types of rebates: fixed (also known as prescriptive) and custom. "Fixed rebates make the lives of everybody involved easier. They are adjusted annually and based on a variety of factors like account type, technology trends and the energy conservation measure (ECM) itself such as lighting or solar. Any provider, whether they are on the approved contractor list or not, and any account holder, can easily complete the fixed rebate application on the website and submit. 60-90 days later, the rebate check will arrive.

Take a standard lighting replacement for example, if you remove one kind of lamp and install a new one, that is *approved* for a fixed rebate, you simply complete the fixed rebate application then receive a rebate check. Some lamps have a five-dollar rebate and others have a $250 rebate. The factors that determine the rebate amount are wattage, cost, efficiency, etc. Another good example of a fixed rebate is solar. For every solar panel installed that *qualifies* for a rebate, there is a $500 fixed rebate per solar panel."

"Just to confirm, when you say lamps that are 'approved' for a rebate, you mean they are on the DLC QPL, correct?" Joe asks.

"Yes Joe. I'm surprised you know that. Also, some lighting fixture types, technically known as luminaires, like decorative wall sconces, do not qualify for rebates under our programs. The last thing we want to incentivize is installing aesthetically pleasing lights regardless of whether they are energy efficient or not."

"That makes sense," Joe confirms.

Mary continues, "Custom rebates, on the other hand, are more complex. ECMs that are unique and difficult to quantify in terms of energy savings and are not categorized in the fixed rebate program, *might* qualify for a custom rebate. Think of the complexities involved with installing two high efficiency boilers in the place of one old boiler for example or the challenges of installing a completely new lighting system for a warehouse that uses half of the number of existing luminaires. These are custom ECM's that do not fit into the fixed rebate programs.

It is difficult to quantify the energy savings for these. An approved contractor needs to be involved to obtain the rebate. His engineers need to calculate energy savings and submit them to an engineer here at the utility company for review. An inspection of the facility also needs to be completed both prior to and after the improvements are made.

Finally, the utility bill needs to be monitored for a period of time after installation to ensure the improvement is saving the energy it was engineered to save; this is known as measurement and verification (M&V).

Usually, the custom rebate amounts are a fixed dollar amount per unit of energy saved, or a percentage of the total project cost ($0.25/kWh saved or 25% of the total project cost for example).

Joe, are the two providers you've received proposals from on the approved contractors list?"

"Yes, they both are," Joe confirms.

"Good. The process for you is going to be very easy. After

you agree to the improvements, the providers will send you the rebate applications, pre-populated for each improvement. Simply sign and send them back to the two providers. We'll work with them directly to process the applications and mail you the rebate checks within 90 days of the project completion dates."

"Wow, that's really straightforward," Joe says. "But how do I know if the rebates on the proposals are fixed or custom? Do I just assume they are fixed?

Mary replies, "First, you can cross-reference the rebate amounts on the proposals with those listed on our website. You can also ask the provider or reverse engineer the rebates. Once you're a little more familiar with the rebate programs in terms of which improvements have fixed rebates and which are custom, you'll quickly be able to identify the difference.

There is a lot of trust involved too. You'll have to trust that the providers' savings and rebate totals are accurate, unless you have your own independent advisor working for you."

"That's a good point. Thanks, Mary!"

Joe continues, "I'd like to play devil's advocate for a minute. Are there ever any instances in which providers overestimate the savings and rebates on their proposals and a customer has the project installed and obtains only a very small amount of energy savings and rebate money?"

"Joe," says Mary, "I would be lying to you if I said that never happens. It does. That is why I'm happy to hear you are taking the time to perform the cautious review you are.

Hiring a third party, such as the company I just shared with you, to review the proposals is always a good idea. Most people don't have the time, discipline or resources to do what you are doing. Some providers take advantage of that. Others simply make a mistake or two in their estimations.

In some cases, thousands of dollars are left on the table because the savings and rebates are too conservative. Other times, the opposite is true, and the customers are bewildered when they don't see any savings and receive a very small rebate check, or none at all.

It's always difficult for me to field these calls and explain why the proposed rebate was not approved, especially after they've signed an agreement and are on the hook to pay the balance."

"That's eye opening," Joe replies, as he thinks back to the new construction rebate oversight on his restaurant build outs.

"If you don't mind me asking, Joe, who are the two providers you are considering working with?"

Joe happily shares the names of both companies hoping to gain Mary's approval.

She reassures him that he is in good hands and she has spoken to many utility account holders who have had great experiences working with them.

Appreciative of Mary's help, Joe thanks her and tries to end the phone call when Mary jumps in with another question, "How are you planning to pay for the improvements?"

Taken aback by her question and knowing he doesn't have an answer, he responds, "That's a good question. We don't have any allocated funds so I'm probably going to explore whatever financing options my bank offers. Hopefully, they'll have something that makes sense."

"The reason I ask, Joe, is we do have an on-bill financing

program for businesses like yours. Would you like to hear about it?"

Looking at his clock, Joe sees he needs to end the call or he'll be late for an all hands staff meeting. He tells Mary that he is interested but needs to go. "Could you email me the information?"

"Absolutely. Give us a call back if you have any other questions."

After thanking Mary, Joe hangs up and gets ready for his meeting.

# ASPECT 5: INCENTIVES AND TAX CREDITS - PART 2

After his morning meeting and a busy lunch rush, Joe heads into his restaurant office to review Mary's email with the on-bill financing information. Upon opening his inbox, he sees an email from the local Chamber of Commerce announcing a new grant program for energy efficiency improvements.

Curious, he opens the email and learns the town has received state funds to subsidize the cost of qualifying energy efficiency improvements for single location storefront businesses less than a year old.

"Damn," he says, knowing he does not qualify for the program.

Interested in seeing if there are any other grant programs available that he *does* qualify for, he visits the town's website and pokes around for a few minutes. There are grant programs, but none he qualifies for at the moment.

He also visits the Database of State Incentives for Renewables & Efficiency's website, http://www.dsireusa.org/, as Mary suggested, but comes up empty handed.

Already distracted, he flags Mary's email to review later and takes out the two proposals. With the information Mary has given him, Joe is well prepared to verify the rebate amounts on the proposals are in sync with what is available to him from the utility company.

He pulls up each corresponding rebate program on the utility company's website and verifies that the rebate amount on the proposal matches.

He also makes sure to read the fine print on both proposals which states, "rebates listed are estimates, not guarantees" and "provider will handle application filing at no additional cost."

This matches Mary's statement that the utility company has the final say in the rebate amounts paid out. Both providers will make his life easy by filing the rebate applications for him.

Satisfied that every penny of utility rebate money available to him is indeed included in the two proposals, Joe is pleased with his progress.

On cue, his phone begins to ring. Although he doesn't recognize the number, he picks it up anyway. Usually that's a bad idea but today he has a different outcome.

Lisa, the sales manager from the walk-in cooler controls company, is on the other end, calling to see if he has any questions after reviewing the proposal.

Joe fills her in on his verification process, informing her that most of his questions have already been answered. He takes the opportunity to ask her a question off the record. It's a question related to his experience in the banking industry.

He politely asks if during her career in the energy efficiency business, she has known of any providers bending the rules of the utility rebate programs. Has she met any who compromise on ethics to move the needle more in their favor?

Her hesitancy in answering the question gives Joe his answer. Joe affirms however, that he is not suspecting her referrals of being unethical. He is simply looking for an honest perspective, off the record, to try and understand the inner workings of the industry.

He proceeds to share a story with her from his experience in banking. On one occasion, a competing bank loaned money to businesses that lacked the creditworthiness his bank required. When a high percentage of the loans defaulted, a Securities and Exchange Commission (SEC) investigation ensued in which the competitor was exposed.

With this she responds as Joe had hoped. She informs him that some providers take the utility rebates for themselves. If done honestly, this simply saves the customer from unnecessary paperwork and allows for a cost discount equal to the rebate amount. Sometimes, however, providers only discount the project cost by a *percentage* of the total rebate and take the difference as extra profit. Uninformed customers don't know they're not receiving the total rebate discount because it's all behind the scenes. They naïvely trust the provider to do the right thing and don't understand the rebate programs in general. Depending on the size of the project, thousands of dollars could be left on the table in these cases.

Lisa continues, "I once saw a salesperson at a competing firm develop a project that lost money. He made too many incorrect and inaccurate assumptions up front and his compensation was affected. On the next project he developed, he padded the profit by telling the utility company that his customer didn't want the hassle of dealing with the rebate and instead preferred a discounted price, a discount which he never included. The customer, unbeknownst to him, approved the project without any discount whatsoever. The provider received the rebate check and the salesman made up his earlier loss with a very high commission on the second project.

Engaging in a business practice like that is not only unethical, but if the utility company catches wind of it, the provider could be permanently banned from participating in the rebate programs. These rebate programs generate a lot of business for approved contractors. Many rely heavily on these for their revenue streams."

Thanking her for her honesty Joe switches gears. He informs her of his financial situation. He doesn't have any allocated budget for the improvement. To move forward, he will need to finance the project. He tells her he just learned about the utility company's on-bill financing program and asks if that is a payment option for the walk-in cooler controls improvement.

To his surprise, she confirms that yes, the on-bill financing program is an option. For larger projects with a total cost over $10,000, other financing options are available such as capital equipment leases. But, due to the small size of this improvement alone, it is not an option in this case.

The conversation pivots as Joe informs her of his plan to bundle all four improvements together if he can find a way to finance them. If he can do that, he'll be making his decision within the next week or so.

She agrees to follow up with him and they end the conversation.

# ASPECT 6: PAYMENT OPTIONS – PART 1

Later that evening, after returning home from the restaurant, Joe decides it would be a good time to catch up with an old colleague from his former bank, Bob Jones.

Bob was one of the regional managers and had worked in the commercial banking industry for years. He was well in-tune with the lending options available for all types of business needs.

Joe reaches Bob on his way home from the office, stuck in traffic. After catching up for a few minutes, he begins explaining his situation, informing Bob of the energy efficiency improvements he is considering. He talks about the tax incentives available, the valuation increase the improvements will have on his restaurant, and the fact that he has zero allocated budget for the $30,000 cost.

Bob begins by refreshing Joe's memory of the ways they used to finance build outs, remodels and HVAC improvements: extended lines of credit and small business loans. "As I'm sure you remember, the lines of credit often had very high interest rates and were intended for day-to-day operational needs. Even if a business could get approved for a large line of credit, holding a balance for an extended period resulted in an enormous amount of interest to pay. As far as small business loans are concerned, the time and paperwork required to get a loan approved were prohibitive in and of themselves, not to mention the need to put up collateral or a personal guarantee."

Joe recalls the legwork necessary to process them. "I remember processing those loans. They often took months to finalize. I spent most of my time chasing documents back and forth."

"I'm happy to inform you," says Bob," they are no longer the only options. With the boom in energy efficiency, financing these improvements has become such a big opportunity for lenders so they have gotten creative. I recently attended a conference that was explaining the details of 'Energy Service Agreements' (ESA) and 'Managed Energy Service Agreements' (MESA)."

"Could you explain those to me?" Joe asks.

"Sure. First off, I wouldn't recommend either option. Since you want to use the tax incentives to offset both the implementation cost and the new tax expenses that will result from the valuation increase, you won't be able to capture those incentives with these agreements but, here's the rundown.

With ESA's and MESA's, the providers fund the cost of completing the improvements, so there is no up-front cost to you. You repay them monthly for a period from the energy savings the improvements generate. During this period, the providers often maintain the equipment and monitor the savings for you.

Another benefit is that payments made can be accounted for as operational expenses, off your balance sheet, keeping your debt-to-equity ratio low.

But, until you've paid back the provider, you do not own the equipment. And, the repayment terms will vary based on a several factors, like energy savings and total cost.

But, once you've paid back the provider, there is usually a buy-out option in which you can buy the equipment at its fair market value.

One danger with these agreements is it's difficult to determine the total cost of the improvements. Sometimes they only list the energy savings and repayment terms so it is tough to know if you are getting a good deal or getting ripped off.

And, seeing the providers are paid back from the energy savings, *their* goal is to obtain the largest amount of energy savings. If *your* goal is to increase the lighting levels in your restaurant for example, you'll need to ensure the project they develop achieves that, which is difficult without being a lighting expert.

There are a lot of other nuances as well so it's critical to have an energy efficiency advisor and your attorney review them. That's the quick overview."

"Interesting," Joe responds. "I can see how these would be useful if I owned a multi-tenant office building where the tenants lease the space and pay the utility bills but I own and operate both the restaurant and the building. So you're right; these options don't sound like they would make the most sense."

"There's another option too that has received a lot of traction over the past few years that might make more sense for you," Bob suggests. "Are you familiar with capital equipment leases?"

"Somewhat," Joe replies, "I recently completed four build-outs and the kitchen equipment vendor was explaining them to me. Apparently, I didn't need to put up any collateral because the equipment itself was the collateral, I would pay a monthly installment just like I would with a loan and I could finance the installation cost as well in addition to the cost of the equipment. Then, at the end of the payment plan, I would own the equipment.

I didn't really see much value in it since the kitchen equipment was just one piece of the full project, so I just financed the whole project through a traditional bank loan."

"Those are the basics," Bob concurs. "Recently, this financing option has become available for energy efficiency improvements. The real benefits of capital equipment leases are how quickly they can be processed, unlike bank loans. Have you ever financed a new car?"

"Yes I have, but what does that have to do with this?"

"It has everything to do with it. A capital equipment lease is essentially a car loan. Remember going to the dealership, having a credit check run, receiving a term sheet showing you your interest rate and term length, then signing and driving off the lot the same day?"

"It took *all day!* I remember that."

Chuckling, Bob continues, "Same day is better than three months from now, right? These leases are quick to execute through a simple process. You don't need to put up collateral or offer a personal guarantee and the best part is the full project cost can be financed including labor and equipment. Once you've made your last lease payment, you own the equipment, just like with a car loan when the title is transferred from the lender to you."

Thinking this sounds too good to be true, Joe replies, "Sounds promising Bob, but what's the catch?"

"The catch is this. With these leases, you typically don't need to put up collateral or offer a personal guarantee. So, if you default on your payments, the lender has no way of being re-paid. Because of this, the interest rates are higher than, say, a home mortgage, where the lender simply forecloses on your house then resells it to somebody else.

To overcome the misperception around higher interest rates, providers offer promotional financing. You see it all over the place: '0% for 72 months'. You and I both know there is no such thing as free money."

"So, to offer 0% interest, they increase the total cost to pay the interest rate down to '0', right?" Joe asks.

"Exactly," Bob replies. "Which is unfortunate when you want to pay cash because the price is still the same. Instead of interest being pre-paid, the provider just makes a whole lot of extra profit. If you are going to consider a capital equipment lease, I would recommend the standard interest rate over the promotional interest rate. That way you can write off the interest payments on your tax return."

Joe thanks Bob and ends their call. Hopeful that he will find a payment option that meets his needs, Joe wraps up his work in time to have dinner with his wife and daughter.

After dinner, Joe returns to his home office and opens Mary's follow-up email. It contains a link to the on-bill financing (OBF) program. He clicks to learn more.

Through spending a half hour reading about the program, Joe learns quite a bit. First, he learns the interest rate is 0%. He finds the utility company can offer no-interest repayment terms not because they increase the total cost or decrease the total rebates, rather, because a portion of the pool of money collected from the Energy Conservation charges is set aside in case there is a default.

He also learns how to opt-in to the OBF program, simply by letting the providers know before he signs their agreements, that he is electing to pay through OBF. By doing so, the providers can invoice the utility company first and then charge the customer for the repayments on their utility bill. All *he* must do is sign an acknowledgement form authorizing this prior to installation.

Repayment charges will commence a month after the improvements are installed. Both Joe and the approved contractor will sign a Project Completion Form acknowledging the improvements are complete to both of their satisfaction, allowing the contractor to invoice the utility company and the utility company to begin charging Joe.

Joe learns from reading the FAQ's about the OBF program that although it is only available for improvements with an associated rebate, "a project developed by an approved contractor which includes three or more ECMs with two or more of those ECMs qualifying for rebates, qualify for the OBF program." This is a relief in terms of the rooftop unit improvement which does not have a rebate *but* is part of the ECM project developed by Mike's company.

Upon reading the repayment terms for the program, Joe becomes concerned. The program only allows a maximum term of 36 months and the cumulative payback of all four improvements is exactly that length of time. This means, that if Joe moves forward with the improvements and uses OBF, he will not save any money on his utility bill for the next three years. He will only break even.

Deciding it best to sleep on it and review what payment options are mentioned in both Mike's and the walk-in cooler controls proposals in the morning, Joe shuts down his computer and begins winding down for the night.

# ASPECT 6: PAYMENT OPTIONS – PART 2

The next morning, he sits down again at his home office and begins reviewing the two proposals. Feeling confident he is getting close to making his decision and happy he's followed through on investigating the opportunities, he sees the light at the end of the tunnel.

First, he scans the walk-in cooler proposal and quickly notices the on-bill financing option just as it was advertised on the utility company's website.

The other payment option listed is a cash option, with the following terms: "25% due upon signing and the balance due upon substantial completion of the work."

"What the hell does 'substantial completion' mean?" Joe thinks to himself. "Oh, I remember this one from the build-outs. It's when the work is 'sufficiently complete so that I can use it for its intended purposes.'"

Although he doesn't have the cash to use this option, he considers these terms a little further. If there is a punch list of outstanding items, they can still invoice me. And if I pay the invoice prior to the punch list being completed, I lose all leverage in having it completed. This is a mistake he made with the first build-out. A sub-contractor left some trash and extra material in his storage room and it was like pulling teeth to get it removed after paying their final invoice.

"I guess the terms of the OBF program are better for me anyhow, seeing the repayment charges will not commence until I sign the Project Completion Form, after the punch list is complete," he reflects. "Plus, I don't have any funds left to even pay the 25% deposit."

With that, he concludes the OBF option is the repayment option he's going to use, if he decides to move forward with the walk-in cooler controls improvement.

Next, he turns to Mike's proposal. Once again, he sees the OBF option just as it was shown on the utility company's website. What he doesn't find is any mention of the leasing options Bob informed him of.

Finding that a bit curious, he considers what options remain *if* the payback of the improvements happened to be five years, over the break-even point of three years at 0% interest through the OBF program.

Unless Mike would be willing to work with both him and an independent lender offering capital equipment leases, which seems like a long shot, his options appear to be limited.

He doesn't have any funds to pay Mike through cash terms and he can't afford any additional charges on his utility bill, which would ensue if the payback was five years with the maximum OBF term of only three years.

He simply wouldn't be able to perform *all* the improvements at once, at least not through Mike's company. He would either have to phase the improvements over several years, completing one at a time starting with the highest ROI improvement to grow a revolving fund from the energy savings. He could then use this to complete the next improvement. Or, he can decline the proposal and find a provider offering capital equipment leases. This seems like an enormous waste of time considering how far he's come with Mike.

It's strange, he thinks, that more providers don't offer multiple repayment options considering nearly every other industry does! Cars, houses, groceries, appliances can all be paid for in a variety of ways.

Joe assumes Mike's company does not offer ESA's or MESA's, because they are not listed on the proposal so he writes a note to ask Mike if there are any other repayment options. Having come this far, he reasons, it would be a disservice not to ask, just in case.

He then reads Mike's cash repayment terms just in case, "50% due upon signing, 25% due upon substantial completion and the remaining balance due upon customer sign-off at project completion." Wondering why these terms are more aggressive than those on the walk-in cooler proposal, he writes down another question to ask Mike.

He reaches Mike and informs him of all the progress he's made since they last spoke on Tuesday evening. He fills him in on the conversation with his accountant about tax incentives, the information his former bank colleague provided about capital equipment leases, ESA's and MESA's, the phone call with Mary at the utility company about the rebate programs, and what he's learned about the on-bill financing program.

"Joe, that is really great to hear!" says Mike. "You know, 99% of people simply do not do the homework and inevitably expose themselves to a lot of risks. I can't believe the effort you've put in. You are very invested in making a wise decision here."

"Thanks Mike. I am. Although it's time consuming, confusing and burdensome, I can't afford to make a bad decision on these improvements. I understand why you didn't include any information about the tax incentives - not being an accountant yourself, but the numbers Phillip allowed me to calculate are pretty convincing."

Mike agrees and reiterates that they simply cannot take the risk of including them in their proposals because they are not tax professionals.

Joe proceeds to ask Mike if they offer any other financing options in addition to the OBF program such as capital equipment leases, ESA's and MESA's.

"Unfortunately, no," Mike informs Joe, explaining that his business partner has been quite reluctant to offer financing options.

"We've been in business for 20 years and have done well thus far. He thinks we'll be fine without them." Mike further explains that he doesn't agree with this decision since the competition is increasingly offering financing, taking away from their market share.

He explains their business model was never set up for them. "We would need a large amount of capital to lend against or have to partner with a few lenders to do so." If Joe would like to consider one of these agreements, Mike continues, "I know of a provider I can refer you to."

"In my personal opinion," Mike proceeds, "owner occupied businesses like yours typically get more value out of owning the improvements outright, either by paying cash from an allocated budget or by financing them through a preferred bank that offers capital equipment leases."

"Thank you for your honesty, Mike. I just learned about them and figure I would ask. I don't think an ESA or MESA is the right option. Leasing the improvements might make sense but I'm leaning toward the OBF option. Are there any other options out there?"

"Yes and no. Let me explain. There is an option called <u>PACE, Property Assessed Clean Energy</u>. Here's how it works. It's a new financing option that is attached to the property itself. Repayments occur annually on the property taxes assessed to the owner, whomever that might be. However, if a bank owns the property, they need to approve the assessment. Also, the local government needs to approve the program. Unfortunately, our town has yet to approve PACE so it is not available here yet."

"Interesting. I'll have to read more about it. That might be a useful option in the future," Joe replies. "One last question for you, Mike. Then I'll let you go. I noticed your payment terms are 50% due upon signing, 25% due upon substantial completion, and the remaining balance due upon customer sign-off when the project is fully completed. Those terms are a bit aggressive don't you think? I don't have much cash on hand so I won't be cutting you a check, but the other proposal I am considering has more conservative payment terms. Why are yours more aggressive? And what are the industry norms?"

Mike responds, "Being a contractor, we're at the mercy of the equipment providers with the payment terms we can offer. If they have good payment terms and allow us some time, say 30 days, to pay them for the equipment we buy, then we can pass those terms on to our customers.

For the equipment we're planning to install at your

restaurant, that is not the case. All of the equipment is great but the manufacturers and distributors have tight payment terms. For example, we buy the lighting fixtures from a distributor who ships them to our warehouse and invoices us *in full* upon shipping them. In some cases, we receive the invoice before we receive the lights. For small projects under $5,000, we can be flexible with our payment terms because installation can be completed in a week or two. But on bigger projects that take months to install, we cannot afford the hit to our cash reserves by paying the distributors up front and waiting for our customers to pay us 90 days later after lights are installed. We try to find some middle ground and stage the payments so we don't burden our customers and at the same time can pay our bills. These terms are in-line with industry norms. You'll see a variation of them typically: "25% due upon signing and the balance upon project completion" or "50% due upon signing and the balance upon completion."

Joe assures Mike that he has been a tremendous help. "I've asked a lot of you since you first shared the proposal with me. You've really helped me make sense of this whole thing. And thanks to you, I have a good handle on what's in front of me. I don't have any more questions but need some time to digest everything. Give me a few more days and I'll have a decision."

# DECISION TIME

On Saturday morning, Joe decides to go on a hike, something he enjoys doing before making big decisions. Spending time alone in nature always helps him gain clarity and perspective. It allows him to detach from his busy schedule, to calm his mind enough to make logical and carefully considered, unemotional choices.

When he arrives at the state park, backpack full of snacks and water for the ½ day hike, he is greeted by a warm and sunny autumn day. As he begins on the trail, his mind races as he reviews all the events of the past weeks. From the fire alarm tripping to his products being spoiled in the walk-in cooler to the bullet he dodged when he avoided signing the HVAC company's proposal before the energy efficiency audit was performed, he considers every little twist and turn.

As he continues down the trail, he considers the lessons he learned at the bank and how he carried them over to the build outs. He reflects on how he felt when he quit his bank job and bought the burger business – nervous yet excited. He thinks about the time and energy it took to go from where he was five years ago to where he is now. His wife and daughter come to mind as he considers how the business demands have taken away from his abilities to spend time with them, to do the fun activities that he enjoys, like taking hikes and attending his daughter's sporting events.

After two hours of hiking through the forest, he reaches a scenic overlook and pauses for a few minutes to rest and have a snack. While he enjoys the view, he reflects on his original objective - to explore the anomaly he found while reviewing last year's financial statements. The potential opportunity, a 15% reduction in utility expenses, equal to $9,000 per year, would allow the original restaurant to operate at the same efficiency as the four newest locations.

Joe replays everything he's done to explore the opportunity: all the time he dedicated to his research efforts, the pitfalls he avoided, the conversations with Mike, what he's learned about energy efficiency providers, equipment, energy and O&M savings, assumptions that are often made, the financial metrics to consider, the environmental benefits, utility rebates and tax incentives, and the variety of payment terms and payment options. He reflects on just how much there is to know and learn to make a well-informed business decision on energy efficiency improvements.

In thinking about this, he asks himself why he set the goal he did. Was it really about improving his operating efficiency or was it something bigger? He remembers all the values he wrote down that were important to him. Remembering that initially he was quite naïve, thinking it was only about the money he could save, he realizes it was about much more. It was about eliminating the headaches and emergency repair costs draining his time, energy, and bank account. These headaches were driving away customers and reducing employee morale. It was about not being able to attend his daughter's softball games or family dinners and when he did, not having the energy or peace of mind to enjoy family time together. It was about improving food presentation and attracting new customers, making his business more valuable, and improving safety and comfort in his restaurant.

He realizes that even if he only breaks even over the next few years (a conservative prediction considering rising energy costs), preserving these values will be worth it.

He knows deep down his decision has been made. Come Monday morning, he's going to sign both proposals, opt in to the OBF program, and move forward with all four energy efficiency improvements.

But for now, he's going to enjoy the rest of the hike carefree and relaxed, knowing he's made a wise investment decision.

# CONCLUSION

One month after the installation of all four energy efficiency improvements, Mike stops by the restaurant to grab lunch and check in with Joe. Thrilled with the results and excited to see him, Joe treats Mike to a free lunch as a gesture of his appreciation. Once the two sit down, Joe is quick to show Mike his most recent utility bill while lunch is being prepared.

"Looks like your bill is down more than 18%," Mike responds after taking a look.

"Better than projected, Mike! And you know what? Revenue is up more than 20%! And how about our display on the front lawn?"

Joe and his managers decided the improvements would make a great advertising campaign to attract new eco-minded customers. They rented a massive inflatable lawn display to showcase their commitment to reducing their carbon footprint.

"Love it!" Mike replies.

"After you sent the $CO_2$ savings, we decided it would make for a great visual. So, I contacted an inflatable party supply company to rent this 27-cubic foot display! We had the banner made to communicate exactly *why* we have this on the lawn."

Mike reads the banner hung across the top, "Our eco-friendly improvements prevent this much $CO_2$ from entering our air."

"People love it! And the kids love jumping in it."

"That's really creative. I'm happy you are getting the most out of the improvements. It sounds like the energy savings was just the beginning!"

As they walk back inside to have lunch, Joe elaborates on the results he is realizing.

"Because the improvements are performing better than projected, we are cash-flow positive, despite the OBF payments. With the increase in business, we are doing a lot better than we were two months ago. The installers did a great job training us on the basic O&M required to keep the controls systems running at peak efficiency. They did A+ work and didn't interrupt our business operations at all. We've had an increase in online reviews touting the atmosphere in our restaurant and the food presentation - direct results of installing the new rooftop units, kitchen hood controls and lights. At night, the exterior really glows, attracting an influx of customers for dinner.

My staff is more productive and comfortable too. I can tell they're happy with the improvements just based on their mood and the decrease in turnover. They're having more fun. They see I've invested in the business and want to reciprocate the efforts.

But the best part Mike, is I haven't worked from home in weeks. I've been able to get my family life back. I'm spending more time with my wife and daughter, sleeping better and enjoying being a business owner again. The freedom these improvements have afforded me has been priceless. I never would have imagined this would be the outcome."

As they eat and continue to converse, Mike enjoys the feeling of accomplishment in a job well done, knowing this is why he does what he does. His greatest satisfaction is helping people like Joe achieve their goals by using energy efficiency as a business strategy.

Reflecting on all the benefits that result from something as simple as an energy efficiency improvement project, he thinks it's a shame more people don't move forward with these projects. He knows the obstacles are plentiful but he wishes he could convince others of the wisdom of the investment.

He recognizes the common resistances: lack of time and know-how to do the investigative work, lack of trust in predicted savings and in technology, bad experiences in the past with oversights, inaccurate assumptions, or poor quality projects.

He wonders if there is a way he can direct his customers to a resource to provide the research and evaluation that is so demanding. What is needed is an industry expert who can evaluate projects and educate clients so more of them move forward with business-building proposals and realize the power of energy improvements firsthand.

He turns his attention back to Joe who is still flying high and praising the improvements that have so enhanced his business and his quality of life.

# EPILOGUE

The framework I've provided to you through Joe's story will allow you to sort through the options in the marketplace so you can navigate the six aspects of energy efficiency projects successfully and make wise investment decisions.

I've pointed out and discussed each of these aspects as well as some common pitfalls and shortcuts. I've brought to light the common and critical but not-so-apparent project details such as the methodologies and assumptions used to develop energy savings, the financial and non-financial benefits, the availability of utility rebates and tax incentives, and the financing options available.

With the blueprint I've provided, you can walk through the process competently as you successfully navigate the energy efficiency marketplace.

My hope is that, like Joe, you've learned something in this process. Although Joe had some prior experience in the banking industry and owns his own business, these are by no means prerequisites for making the most out of energy efficiency improvements. The development and evaluation of energy efficiency projects is complex. While Joe took the arduous process upon himself, I recommend utilizing the expert resources now available to you.

While there are a variety of energy efficiency professionals and companies that specialize in energy improvement, please consider Energy Project Advisors, an independent resource you can rely on. We have no financial ties to contractors, equipment manufacturers, utility companies, lenders, or government agencies.

Most industries utilize companies that independently review, appraise, assess, and qualify the critical aspects in the buying process. In the used car industry, consumers rely on unbiased accident history reports to determine the integrity of the vehicles they are considering purchasing. In the real estate market, consumers rely on independent inspections and appraisals to insure their money will be well spent. Energy Project Advisors provides the same service in the energy efficiency industry, specializing in screening providers, reviewing energy audits, and, most importantly, grading proposals. We offer these services to give clients like you the insight and information needed to make wise investment decisions.

Whether you decide to utilize our services or not, I hope this book achieves its goal of renewing your trust in the benefits of energy improvements, alleviating confusion and skepticism, and providing a framework for you to tackle your challenges with increased confidence. You now have what it takes to evaluate a proposal, increase the probability of exceeding its projections, significantly reduce your risks, and make wise investment decisions.

# ENERGY PROJECT ADVISORS

Jeff started Energy Project Advisors with the vision of creating a trusted resource for buyer representation on energy efficiency projects and eliminating the skepticism these projects often face. In his years of working in the commercial energy efficiency industry on nearly $500M of projects, Jeff identified an urgent need for transparency and trustworthiness in the business. He recognized that business clients need an unbiased liaison and founded Energy Project Advisors to become that valued intermediary resource.

"The energy efficiency industry, loaded with self-proclaimed experts, is built on the need to convince a customer to move forward with an efficiency project in which the seller has an economic interest. As an independent buyer's representative, my goal is to educate clients, enabling them to make the most appropriate energy investment for their needs and dollars."

To contact Energy Project Advisors, please visit our website, www.energyprojectadvisors.com, give us a call at 512-765-5328 or send us an email at info@energyprojectadvisors.com.

# JEFF JULIA

# ABOUT THE AUTHOR

Jeff Julia is a subject matter expert, engineer, author and advisor focused on sharing his insider experience with professionals of all kinds to promote understanding, trust and business success.

He is the founder Energy Project Advisors which serves as an objective advisory firm assessing the integrity and validity of energy saving proposals.

Previously, Jeff worked with Noesis Energy after moving to Austin, TX from Boston, MA in 2015. There, he collaborated with a wide range of energy efficiency providers and utility companies such as Digital Lumens, Service Logic, Thermal Mechanics and Pacific Gas & Electric to support their business development teams with financial modeling and presentation strategy as an energy project consultant.

In Boston, Jeff actively developed energy efficiency projects for a wide range of clients including the Commonwealth of Massachusetts, Brown University, Babson College, Clark University, Worcester Polytechnic Institute (WPI), John Hancock, Ariad Pharmaceuticals and Angell Animal Medical Center.

With RISE Engineering, Jeff partnered with local utility companies, Eversource and National Grid, to provide his clients with the most impactful and beneficial projects that achieved their goals. His clients included non-profits, colleges, industrial businesses, biotech firms, multi-tenant office buildings, retail stores and restaurants amongst others.

He began his career in energy engineering and project management with GreenerU on a wide variety of unique energy efficiency projects.

Jeff holds a B.S. in Mechanical Engineering from Northeastern University's acclaimed College of Engineering while minoring in Business Administration.

Jeff lives in Austin, TX with his wife Abby.

To learn more about the tools and services his firm provides, visit www.energyprojectadvisors.com

(for businesses) or www.efficiencyinsider.com (for homeowners).

# GLOSSARY

Change Order – a document that details a change required to the scope of work agreed upon by the provider and customer

Commercial – commerce based building or business

Cost Segregation – the practice of identifying and classifying assets and their costs for tax purposes

Cut Sheet – also called "spec sheet" provides detailed information of the product/equipment being proposed

Energy Conservation Measure (ECM) – a type of project or technology that reduces energy consumption

Energy Efficiency – using less energy to produce the same outcome

Energy Efficiency Audit Report – a written document describing the current use of and condition of energy consuming systems and equipment, typically resulting in a visit to the building or business by a provider

Energy Savings – future avoided consumption of energy and outflow of cash resulting from a project, typically over the course of one year

Incentive – see Rebate

Rebate – also called "incentive", is a sum of money utility companies pay-back to their customers for installing energy efficient equipment

Measurement & Verification (M&V) – the process of quantifying the energy saved by an energy conservation measure

Personal Guarantee – a written promise from a business owner guaranteeing payment on an equipment lease or loan in the event the business does not pay

Project – an improvement to the infrastructure of a building

Proposal – written offer describing the details of a suggested project

Provider – salesperson or company responsible for creating the proposal

Scope of Work – the details of the project as described in the proposal